MW00813077

Modesty
THE MISSING GEM

Dorothy Zimmerman

Modesty
THE MISSING GEM

Dorothy Zimmerman

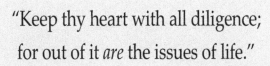

"Keep thy heart with all diligence;
for out of it *are* the issues of life."

– Proverbs 4:23

Table of Contents

Beginning the Journey   9

Lesson 1.   The Designers' Tactics   11

Lesson 2.   Cosmetics for True Beauty   21

Lesson 3.   A Mirror of the Heart   31

Lesson 4.   Is Legalism Legal? Part 1   41

Lesson 5.   Is Legalism Legal? Part 2   53

Lesson 6.   BLURRED VISION   61

Lesson 7.   The Immoral Woman   73

Lesson 8.   The Unfaithful Wife   81

Lesson 9.   Character Clothing   93

Lesson 10.   Women of Character   101

Lesson 11.   The Virtuous Woman   113

Lesson 12.   S e p a r a t i o n   125

Lesson 13.   Eye Magnets   135

Lesson 14.   God's Purpose for Clothing   149

The End of the Journey   157

About the Author   161

Endnotes   163

Bibliography   167

Beginning the Journey

As a teenager in the 1960s, I innocently wore some of the immodest fashions of the culture. I became a Christian at the age of nineteen but was still naïve concerning modesty. A few years later, I learned that the Bible applied to every area of my life, including my wardrobe. I realized that modesty was more than a strict adherence to a set of rules; modesty was a matter of the heart. Henceforth, I resolved to wear clothing that would reflect my love for the Lord and testify to God's working in my heart and life.

The purpose of this Bible study is to encourage women to have the gem of modesty in their life. Perhaps there are women who have never had the opportunity to learn the biblical principles of modesty, or maybe they dismissed the idea for fear of looking unfashionable. Some women may have been given a legalistic view of modesty that caused them to discard the gem. Still, other women have been taught that God does not look at the outward appearance — only the heart. Regardless of a woman's past experience or present opinion about modesty, this study is designed to challenge women to obey the Word of God instead of following the fads and fashions of the culture.

Modesty, The Missing Gem has 14 lessons. Each lesson includes the following sections.

INTRODUCTION: Decide on thought-provoking ideas.

ILLUSTRATION: Develop the lesson with examples.

INSIGHTS: Discover truth in the Bible.

INSTRUCTION: Discuss pertinent information.

INVESTIGATION: Dig for answers to questions.

IN CONCLUSION: Declare a concept to remember.

This Bible study gives a comprehensive overview of modesty based upon scriptural principles. The relevant illustrations and thought-provoking questions are designed to spark the interest of women of all ages. I trust this study will be a fresh approach to a difficult yet timely subject.

LESSON 1

The Designers' Tactics

Introduction

What tactics have fashion designers used in creating their line of clothing?

Illustration

Emily's heart was set on buying a new dress to wear to her friend's wedding. Her mother and grandmother insisted on going along to help with the selection. When they arrived at the department store, Emily was quick to spot a gorgeous powder blue dress. Anxious to try on the dress, she eagerly made her way to the fitting room.

"Mom, this dress is awesome!" Emily exclaimed as she admired herself in the mirror.

Her mother stared intently at the dress as she scrutinized each detail. Emily could see the questioning look on her mother's face.

"What's wrong, Mom? Don't you like the dress?"

"The color's beautiful, Emily, but I just don't think the dress is modest enough. The bare shoulders are all right, but I don't care for the low neckline. I would never have worn a dress like that at your age. What kind of girl will people think you are?"

"C'mon, Mom, it's just a dress. How can my clothes have anything to do with the kind of girl I am? Besides, the dress looks really cool."

"It sure does look cool," protested Grandmother in a raised tone of voice. "Where's the jacket to cover up those bare shoulders?"

Emily felt embarrassed as she saw women nearby glancing in their direction.

"But this is what all my friends wear," argued Emily. "Who wants to look weird and old-fashioned?"

"Old-fashioned seems fine to me," asserted Grandmother. "I've worn my dresses for years; I don't see anything wrong with them. If you ask me, the styles these days make a dress look like it's half missing."

"Oh, Grandma," Emily cried out in exasperation.

"Now let's calm down," interrupted Emily's mother. "It's obvious we're not going to agree on this dress. We need to look in some other stores."

"But, Mom, this dress is perfect! It's just what I wanted," whined Emily.

"Now Emily, I said we need to look elsewhere. There's a new store that opened last week, and it's just down the street. Let's try that one."

Instruction

Is the type and style of clothing important? A woman may view her clothes as meaningless pieces of material, but in the minds of fashion designers, clothing is not neutral.

Clothing communicates a message without a word being spoken. Fashion designers understand this concept, so they intentionally use certain tactics to communicate their personal values and lifestyles through the line of clothing they design. Four of the tactics they use are skimpiness, tightness, sensuality, and purpose.

Skimpiness reduces the amount of fabric to allow for more of the body to be uncovered. An excellent example of this tactic is the swimsuit. The progression is clearly evident in reviewing the history of swimwear.

In the 19th century, women wore bathing gowns made of wool or flannel to prevent the gowns from becoming transparent when wet. The suit with high necks, long sleeves, and ankle-length skirts covered the entire body. The women sewed weights in the hem of the gown to prevent the garment from floating up and exposing the legs. Modesty definitely ruled over fashion.[1]

A bold event happened in 1907 when Annette Kellerman, an Australian swimmer, walked onto Revere Beach in Massachusetts in a one-piece swimsuit that showed her neck, arms, and lower legs. The police arrested her because, at that time, her exposure was considered indecent. The judge accepted the fact that the suit had been designed for exercise, so he made the stipulation that she wear a skirt until she entered the water.[2]

By 1910 the swimsuit began to shrink in all directions. The arms were uncovered and then the legs up to the midthigh. The neckline was lowered to expose the upper chest. The swimsuit became tighter and no longer camouflaged the contours of the female body.[3]

People were shocked in 1913 when Carl Janzten introduced a two-piece bathing suit to enhance the performance of women competing in the Olympics. The shorts and tight-fitting T-shirt with short sleeves caused a scandal.[4]

Public nudity became a real concern on the beaches in the 1920s. Regulations were enforced by beach censors who used measuring tapes to ensure the swimsuits were the right length. If the swimsuits did not meet the regulations, women were told to leave the beach or be arrested.[5]

The designs of the swimsuit changed even more in the 1930s with the invention of latex and nylon. The stretchy nature of the fabrics allowed the swimsuit to be form-fitting. With the tighter fit, backs were lowered, sleeves disappeared, and the sides became tighter. The tighter fit allowed women to lower the straps to get a better tan.[6]

In 1942, because of the vast amount of fabric needed during World War II, the United States War Production Board issued Regulation L-85 that mandated a 10-percent reduction in the amount of fabric in women's beachwear. To comply with the regulation, swimsuit manufacturers produced two-piece suits with bare midriffs. Exposing the midriff was meant for the beach only and was not allowed elsewhere.[7]

Another major change happened in 1946 when French designer Louis Réard noticed women rolled up the edges of their swimsuits to get a better tan. This inspired him to trim the two-piece swimsuit even more to create the bikini. Controversy arose because people were shocked to see a woman's navel exposed in public for the first time.[8]

Swimwear's uncovering of the body continued its progression in the '60s and '70s with the popularity of string bikinis, stringless bikinis, cut-out swimsuits, and sheer suits. The thong, designed by Rudi Gernreich in 1974, reduced the already skimpy amount of fabric on the woman's buttocks to a bare miminum.[9]

In recent years, modern designs have allowed almost all of the body to be seen in the name of fashionable swimwear. If a woman wants to strip down, plenty of styles are designed just for that purpose. The barer the body the better.

The second tactic the designers use is tightness. Tightness reduces the size of the garment with the goal of emphasizing the female form. The well-known American designer Calvin Klein promoted tightness when he boldly stated, "Jeans are sex. The tighter they are, the better they sell."[10]

Leggings, which have been around for centuries, became tighter with the invention of lycra in 1958 by chemist Joseph Shivers. DuPont created the first pair of lycra leggings in 1959, and the fashion industry rapidly embraced the slim, stretchy pants in the 1960s.[11]

The third tactic the designers use is sensuality. Sensuality changes a functional garment into a provocative one. As Mary Quant, a designer from London, admitted, "I love vulgarity. Good taste is death; vulgarity is life."[12] In the 1960s, she was one of the inventors of the miniskirt, which gave a strong message of sexual availability.

Calvin Klein has promoted sensuality as well with his provocative advertisements. His website reads, "We seek to thrill and inspire our audience while using provocative imagery and striking designs to ignite the senses."[13] His ads are infused with eroticism and consist of models wearing nothing more than Calvin Klein underwear.

The fourth tactic the designers use is purpose, i.e., the desire to promote an attitude or lifestyle through a particular line of clothing. Successful marketing agents recognize that the brands of clothing that sell the best are the ones that have a purpose.

One attitude that the designers have communicated is rebellion. This approach was obvious when British designer Vivienne Westwood announced, "I was just using fashion as a way to express my resistance and to be rebellious."[14] Alexander McQueen, another British designer, expressed his rebellion when he rejected traditional norm and embraced the idea that "fashion should be a form of escapism and not a form of imprisonment."[15]

A rebellious designer creates clothing he knows is unacceptable according to traditional standards. His purpose is to break the mold and create a design that is revolutionary. Below are three examples of rebellious designers from *Vogue*'s slideshow entitled "The Ten Most Rebellious Moments in Fashion."

> For his 1992 collection for Perry Ellis, Marc Jacobs, an American fashion designer, looked to the way cool kids were already dressing on the street. He appropriated thrift-store flannel, frumpy silhouettes, and slouchy dresses for the runways, but his cultural declaration was less than appreciated by his employers. Jacobs was fired, and the *New York Times* called the collection "a mess."
>
> Miuccia Prada, an Italian designer, is arguably fashion's most consistent rebel, often deviating from her own ideas of beauty from the previous season. In 1996, when

15

minimal black sheaths were king, Prada introduced a collection of quirky retro prints in shades of moss and chartreuse. She didn't sugarcoat it; the look was inspired by ugliness. How could a collection inspired by the homeless population in Paris not incite extreme controversy?

John Galliano, a British-Spanish designer, accessorized layers of clothes that looked like newspapers with whiskey bottles and silverware. It was perhaps the most opposed collection of all time, and a list of fashion rebellion would be incomplete without it.[16]

Along with communicating attitudes, the designers have used clothes to convey lifestyles. American designer Tommy Hilfiger explained, "I knew exactly what I wanted to do: I wanted to build some kind of lifestyle brand that was preppy and cool."[17] The well-known American designer Ralph Lauren reaffirmed the concept when he declared, "I don't design clothes; I design dreams."[18]

An immoral designer sends forth a lifestyle message with garments designed to attract onlookers. Alexander McQueen created immoral clothing when he invented the low-rise, crevice-revealing Bumster jeans in 1996. Low-rise jeans sit at least three inches below the navel, and the ultra-low-rise jeans are so low that "the zipper no longer has its traditional function but is simply a display of fashion."[19]

Other designers convey their lifestyle with garments that blur the distinction between men and women. In 1966, French designer Yves Saint Laurent created the Le Smoking tuxedo suit with the purpose of dressing women like men. For his Le Smoking collection, he made a subtle change in the shape and curve of the collar on a man's tuxedo to create a more feminine appearance. The waistline of the suit was curved at the sides to accentuate the woman's shape, and the trousers were made slimmer and longer. This design gave women the option to wear clothes that were normally worn by men. Although the response was negative at first, the tuxedo eventually pioneered the way for "the use of power suits and the pantsuit in modern-day society."[20]

Because of the strategies of the fashion designers, clothing styles that were once loose and functional are now tight and sexy, and clothing that was once designed to cover the body is now designed to emphasize and expose the body. The change has not happened by accident but has been exactly what the designers had in mind. French designer Pierre Cardin summed up the goals of the designers when he admitted, "We undress men and women. We don't dress them anymore."[21]

Investigation

Explain why clothes communicate a message without a word being spoken.

_____

_____

_____

List four methods fashion designers use to promote immodesty. Explain each one.

_____

_____

_____

How has the character and lifestyle of the designers been evident in their line of clothing?

_____

_____

_____

Insights

What thoughts come to mind when you hear the word *modesty*? Legalism? Old-fashioned styles? An infringement on personal rights? A hindrance to self-expression? For many women, the subject of modesty is personal, sensitive, and controversial. In this study, the Bible will be the source for truth. To prepare to receive the Word of God, the following attitudes are important.

A HEART THAT LOVES THE LORD AND EARNESTLY DESIRES TO KNOW THE TRUTH

"And ye shall seek me, and find *me*, when ye shall search for me with all your heart" (Jeremiah 29:13).

"But if from thence thou shalt seek the LORD thy God, thou shalt find *him*, if thou seek him with all thy heart and with all thy soul" (Deuteronomy 4:29).

"Blessed *are* they that keep his testimonies, *and that* seek him with the whole heart" (Psalm 119:2).

"With my whole heart have I sought thee: O let me not wander from thy commandments" (Psalm 119:10).

A MIND THAT IS RECEPTIVE TO THE WORD OF GOD

"And be not conformed to this world: but be ye transformed by the renewing of your mind, that ye may prove what *is* that good, and acceptable, and perfect, will of God" (Romans 12:2).

"And be renewed in the spirit of your mind; And that ye put on the new man, which after God is created in righteousness and true holiness" (Ephesians 4:23–24).

"The meek will he guide in judgment: and the meek will he teach his way" (Psalm 25:9).

A WILL THAT IS OBEDIENT AND
SUBMISSIVE TO GOD

"Give me understanding, and I shall keep thy law; yea, I shall observe it with *my* whole heart" (Psalm 119:34).

"I delight to do thy will, O my God: yea, thy law *is* within my heart" (Psalm 40:8).

"Teach me to do thy will; for thou *art* my God: thy spirit *is* good; lead me into the land of uprightness" (Psalm 143:10).

In Conclusion

Fashion designers have used specific tactics to promote immodesty.

"We undress men and women.

We don't dress them anymore."

– Pierre Cardin

Open My Eyes, That I May See

Open my eyes that I may see
Glimpses of truth Thou hast for me;
Place in my hands the wonderful key
That shall unclasp, and set me free.
Silently now I wait for Thee,
Ready, my God, Thy will to see;
Open my eyes, illumine me, Spirit divine!

Open my ears that I may hear
Voices of truth Thou sendest clear;
And while the wave-notes fall on my ear,
Ev'rything false will disappear.
Silently now I wait for Thee,
Ready, my God, Thy will to see;
Open my ears, illumine me, Spirit divine!

Open my mouth, and let me bear
Gladly the warm truth ev'rywhere;
Open my heart, and let me prepare
Love with Thy children thus to share.
Silently now I wait for Thee,
Ready, my God, Thy will to see;
Open my heart, illumine me, Spirit divine!

— Clara H. Scott

LESSON 2

Cosmetics for True Beauty

Introduction

What is God's definition of beauty?

Illustration

Maria was aware that her complexion needed improvement. Determined not to procrastinate any longer, she resolved to go to the cosmetic counter at the local department store. When she arrived, she was surprised to see the wide variety of makeup colors along with a complete line of cosmetics for any skin concern: oily skin, dry skin, large pores, rosacea, acne, hyperpigmentation, and, of course, wrinkles.

The beauty advisor carefully assessed her skin tone and texture and recommended some suitable products. Maria waited patiently as the makeup was meticulously applied. As soon as the specialist finished, Maria gazed in the mirror to inspect the results.

"I can't believe it! I look ten years younger!" she exclaimed with delight.

However, that night when she cleansed her face, the makeup washed off. Maria looked in the mirror and became disheartened as the unsightly imperfections became visible once again.

Instruction

Do cosmetic products really produce the results they promise? Millions of dollars are spent every year putting the "miracle in a tube" to the test. Unfortunately, all of the miracle products in the world cannot eliminate the effects of aging.

God's cosmetics are completely different because His products will not wash away with soap and water. The beauty He desires a woman to have is called modesty. This beauty displays an attractiveness that all the cosmetic products in the world cannot imitate.

Insights

The apostle Paul assigned one of his closest companions named Timothy to be in charge of the work at Ephesus. Timothy was a young pastor who faced various pressures and conflicts from the church and the surrounding culture. Paul's first letter to Timothy was sent to encourage and counsel him in his pastoral responsibilities. In the letter, Paul gave this instruction on how women should dress and conduct themselves in worship: "In like manner also, that women adorn themselves in modest apparel, with shamefacedness and sobriety; not with braided hair, or gold, or pearls, or costly array; But (which becometh women professing godliness) with good works" (1 Timothy 2:9–10).

Modesty demonstrates a standard of moral behavior that is acceptable, sensible, and suitable. Acceptable dress is appropriate for worship and is not offensive to others. Sensible dress is not extravagant, and suitable dress is orderly, neat, and clean in appearance.

Adorning the body enhances one's beauty or attractiveness. The woman's appearance is most attractive when she displays godliness.

When a Christian woman adorns herself in modest apparel, others will be able to focus on her countenance.

Why is focusing on a woman's countenance important?

_____

_____

_____

Shamefacedness describes a woman who is shy and bashful. She does not behave or dress in a manner that attracts attention because she is content staying within the boundaries of decency. Her reverence and godly fear will restrain her from uncovering her body and becoming shameful.

Why would a woman want to draw attention to her body?

_____

_____

Sobriety refers to a woman who uses self-control to avoid extremes or excesses of any kind. A woman who lacks sobriety is undisciplined, self-indulgent, and unrestrained. She follows the impulses of her flesh, especially in regard to pleasure or idleness. A woman with sobriety, however, uses moderation in her actions and is not frivolous, flaunting, or flirtatious.

What do the words *frivolous, flaunting,* and *flirtatious* mean?

_____

_____

_____

Paul admonished the Christian women not to imitate the hairstyles of the pagans. The pagan women would intertwine bands of gold coins, pearls, and silver wire in their hair as a prideful display of beauty and wealth. Their desire was to gain attention and admiration from others, especially men.

To clarify Paul's instruction, he was not forbidding women to braid or style their hair if done with simplicity. His intention was to warn women against the dangers of overemphasis and excessiveness. An overemphasis on styling the hair could leave little or no time for the preparation of the heart for worship. Excessive styling of the hair could result in a conspicuous hairdo that could cause others to be distracted during worship.

What kinds of hairstyles or treatments could be a distraction in a worship service today?

_____

_____

_____

Costly array includes expensive outfits that are conspicuous and flashy. This type of clothing was worn by wealthy women who desired to provoke jealousy and feelings of inferiority in those who were less fortunate.

Name some specific types of garments that could be considered costly array.

_____

_____

_____

The end of verse 10 states that a woman's life should be characterized by good works. A woman who professes godliness should not resort to the fads and fashions of the world to be attractive. Her beauty should come from her godly character as she demonstrates love and kindness to others.

What are some good works that can be done for others?

_____

_____

_____

In addition, Paul sent a letter to Titus, a pastor in Crete, with instructions for the older women in the church. "The aged women likewise, that *they be* in behaviour as becometh holiness…That they may teach the young women to be sober, to love their husbands…*To be* discreet, chaste…that the word of God be not blasphemed" (Titus 2:3–5).

A sober woman has a sound mind and is serious about God and His Word. She is level-headed and demonstrates wisdom and good judgment, especially in stressful situations.

How can a woman control her thoughts and actions in stressful situations?

_____

_____

_____

The older women were to encourage younger women to love their husbands. A wife demonstrates love for her husband when she saves her body exclusively for him. By dressing modestly, she communicates to her husband that he is the only one who has the right to know her in an intimate way. If a woman is single, she purposes to save her body for her future husband as God provides.

How does immodesty communicate a lack of love for a husband?

_____

_____

_____

In verse 5, the women were challenged *"To be* discreet, chaste…that the word of God be not blasphemed." A woman with discretion has a sound mind that allows her to think clearly and carefully so that she is cautious and wise in her conduct and speech. Because she is aware of her behavior, she conducts herself in a way that does not bring reproach to the name of Christ.

Chaste depicts a woman who is morally pure in thought and conduct. She is innocent, clean, and spotless, like a virgin who is morally blameless. A woman who is chaste protects herself and others from moral defilement by refusing to engage in any sexual activity the Bible prohibits.

Why is moral purity important for a Christian girl or woman?

_____

_____

_____

The last phrase reads, "that the word of God be not blasphemed." Non-Christians are very quick to detect imperfections and inconsistencies and will often judge God and His Word by what they observe in the lives of those who profess to be Christians. Someone coined the saying, "Your life may be the only Bible some people will ever read."

God's reputation is affected either positively or negatively by how Christians live.

What attitudes and actions of Christians cause unbelievers to speak irreverently about God?

_____

_____

_____

What attitudes and actions of Christians cause unbelievers to speak respectfully about God?

_____

_____

_____

Instruction

The Bible teaches that modesty begins in the heart. "Whose adorning let it not be that outward *adorning* of plaiting the hair, and of wearing of gold, or of putting on of apparel; But *let it be* the hidden man of the heart, in that which is not corruptible, *even the ornament* of a meek and quiet spirit, which is in the sight of God of great price" (1 Peter 3:3–4).

A woman who is meek has a gentle and humble spirit that allows her to be submissive to authority. If she lacks this quality, she will be self-assertive, argumentative, belligerent, and contentious. A meek woman trusts in God's power to work through the people and circumstances in her life. She does not resist the hand of God but believes Romans 8:28, which says, "And we know that all things work together for good to them that love God, to them who are the called according to *his* purpose."

In verse 3, Peter did not prohibit women to braid their hair or to wear jewelry. He was cautioning women not to depend upon artificial accessories for beauty. The focus should be on inner character, not external appearance.

Certainly, a woman should not neglect her appearance, nor should she allow her appearance to become her top priority. Beauty should come from the heart based upon her relationship with the Lord and her trust in Him. This kind of beauty is precious to God. Physical beauty fades, but the beauty of the soul will last for eternity.

In Conclusion

A godly character and modest apparel give a woman a beauty that all the best cosmetics and expensive clothing in the world cannot duplicate.

> Physical beauty fades, but the beauty
> of the soul will last for eternity.

I Would Be Like Jesus

Earthly pleasures vainly call me,
I would be like Jesus;
Nothing worldly shall enthrall me,
I would be like Jesus.

Refrain:

Be like Jesus, this my song,
In the home and in the throng;
Be like Jesus, all day long!
I would be like Jesus.

He has broken ev'ry fetter,
I would be like Jesus;
That my soul may serve Him better,
I would be like Jesus.

That in Heaven He may meet me,
I would be like Jesus;
That His words "Well done" may greet me,
I would be like Jesus.

— James Rowe

LESSON 3

A Mirror of the Heart

Introduction

Clothing can be a mirror of the heart. What does this statement mean?

Illustration

The local department store mailed out a full-color advertisement for their gigantic, year-end inventory clearance sale. Debra, Jan, and Mary were all anticipating the upcoming event with the expectation of finding some really great bargains.

On the first day of the sale, all three ladies arrived at the store right when the doors opened. They walked briskly to the women's apparel department and anxiously began to look through the selection of discounted dresses.

Debra was in search of a sexy dress to wear to her boss's farewell party Saturday night. After she glanced at the possibilities, she promptly chose a dress with thin straps and a plunging neckline. She was confident the bright, bold design would attract his attention. "Perfect," she whispered as she paid the cashier.

Jan took her time as she carefully inspected each dress. At last, she noticed a beautiful purple one and knew the color would be perfect to enhance her complexion. After a struggle to get the dress on, Jan glanced in the mirror and knew instantly that the dress was too tight. She headed for the racks again to find a larger size but was unsuccessful. After deliberating for several minutes, she hesitantly laid the dress over her arm and walked to the checkout line.

Mary lingered after the other ladies left because she really needed a couple new dresses to replace her old, tattered ones. She thoroughly looked through the racks one more time in hopes of finding a dress, but nothing suited her. Feeling disappointed, she walked to her car and drove away.

Instruction

The three ladies had different outcomes from their shopping trip even though they looked through the same selection of dresses. To understand the reason, consideration must be given to the goals, ambitions, and desires of the heart to determine how they affect a woman's choices.

A goal is determined by a target or desired outcome that a person envisions to accomplish within a certain timeframe. The goal can be observed and measured, which allows the person to verify that their objective has been reached.

Ambition is evidenced by a strong desire and steadfast determination to achieve success. To be successful, a person must possess the motivation to begin, the determination to continue, and the commitment to finish.

A desire motivates a person to hope that an expectation will be fulfilled. If the desire is weak and the expectation is unmet, little disappointment is felt. In contrast, when the desire is strong and the needs and demands are not satisfied, great frustration or even anger could result. When the desire is strong, words like *crave, greed,* and *lust* are used.

Crave indicates a strong desire of the heart. Greed develops when a selfish desire becomes so intense that making it happen becomes an overwhelming impulse, and lust results when an extremely intense and uncontrolled desire becomes a habit.

Debra's goal was to find a dress that looked sexy. Her goal was probably reached quickly because several dresses met the criteria, and modesty was not a concern.

Jan's ambition was to be attractive. She deliberated longer because the dress she chose did not fit properly. The emotional struggle she experienced indicated she had a stronger conviction about modesty than Debra but not as strong as Mary.

Mary's desire was to please the Lord in each decision. After she had carefully examined the selection, she chose not to make a purchase. Although she really needed some new dresses, she decided to leave rather than compromise her strong convictions. Mary believed if she could not find any dresses at this sale, God would provide in another way.

Mary's convictions were based upon the exhortation to "Keep thy heart with all diligence; for out of it *are* the issues of life" (Proverbs 4:23). Guarding and protecting the heart requires a daily deliberate action, as opposed to passive complacency. If a woman is negligent in protecting her heart, she can easily become complacent.

A complacent person has a sense of security that ignores actual danger or deficiency. A woman who is complacent often fails to detect Satan's strategies to turn her heart away from God. Because Satan knows a woman's vulnerability, she must be vigilant against his attempts to deceive.

A diligent person remains steadfast and persistent in reaching a goal— even in the face of opposition and exhaustion. A soldier cannot quit in the middle of a fierce battle, neither can a Christian cease in the fight against Satan. Protection of the heart should be a woman's utmost priority regardless of the cost. Only when the heart is protected will a woman be able to remain on the right path.

The moral conduct of a life is primarily determined by the heart. If the heart is guarded, a pleasant disposition, kind words, and godly actions will likely follow. If the heart is not guarded, uncontrolled tempers, harsh words, or cruel actions could occur. Guarding the heart is of prime importance because the heart affects all of life.

Investigation

All three ladies looked through the same selection of dresses. Why were the outcomes different?

_____

_____

_____

What are some specific ways a woman can guard her heart?

_____

_____

_____

Instruction

If a Christian woman allows her mind to be in control, she may have these thoughts:

"Does it really matter what I wear?"

"All this fuss about dress doesn't make any sense to me."

"Where's the chapter and verse that state this?"

"It's the man's problem, not mine."

If a Christian woman allows her will to be in control, she may struggle with these attitudes:

"Nobody's going to tell me what to wear."

"I have the right to choose my own outfits."

"I refuse to go out and buy new clothes."

"It's my body, and I can look the way I want."

If a Christian woman allows her emotions to be in control, she may experience these feelings:

"I feel comfortable in what I am wearing."

"I don't want to look weird around my friends."

"I like the clothes I picked out, and I don't want to change."

"I'm just not convicted about this."

Insights

When a woman is not a Christian, her mind, will, and emotions will naturally be influenced by the world's philosophies and values. For this reason, she may not hesitate to wear the clothes she chooses even if they are immodest.

The woman who is a believer has the Holy Spirit within her, but she still has a decision to make. She can either obey the Word of God, or she can yield to the selfish desires of her flesh. The outcome will be determined by how faithfully she guards her heart. If she guards her heart, she will want to resist what her flesh tells her, and she will desire to obey the Word of God. If she does not guard her heart, she can easily be deceived by Satan through her mind, will, and emotions.

Investigation

"Search me, O God, and know my heart: try me, and know my thoughts: And see if *there be any* wicked way in me, and lead me in the way everlasting" (Psalm 139:23–24).

"Shew me thy ways, O LORD; teach me thy paths. Lead me in thy truth, and teach me: for thou *art* the God of my salvation; on thee do I wait all the day" (Psalm 25:4–5).

"Let not sin therefore reign in your mortal body, that ye should obey it in the lusts thereof. Neither yield ye your members *as* instruments of unrighteousness unto sin: but yield yourselves unto God, as those that are alive from the dead, and your members *as* instruments of righteousness unto God" (Romans 6:12–13).

According to the previous verses, how can a Christian woman allow the Holy Spirit to have control of her mind, will, and emotions?

_____

_____

_____

_____

How do the goals, ambitions, and desires of a woman's heart affect her clothing choices? Her response to teaching regarding modesty?

_____

_____

_____

_____

Insights

> And the Lord said unto Samuel, How long wilt thou mourn for Saul, seeing I have rejected him from reigning over Israel? Fill thine horn with oil, and go, I will send thee to Jesse the Beth-lehemite: for I have provided me a king among his sons. And Samuel said, How can I go? If Saul hear *it*, he will kill me. And the Lord said, Take an heifer with thee, and say, I am come to sacrifice to the Lord. And call Jesse to the sacrifice, and I will shew thee what thou shalt do: and thou shalt anoint unto me *him* whom I name unto thee. And Samuel did that which the Lord spake, and came to Beth-lehem. And the elders of the town trembled at his coming, and said, Comest thou peaceably? And he said, Peaceably: I am come to sacrifice unto the Lord: sanctify yourselves, and come with me to the sacrifice. And he sanctified Jesse and his sons, and called them to the sacrifice. And it came to pass, when they were come, that he looked on Eliab, and said, Surely the Lord's anointed *is* before him. But the Lord said unto Samuel, Look not on his countenance, or on the height of his stature; because I have refused him: for *the Lord seeth* not as man seeth; for man looketh on the outward appearance, but the Lord looketh on the heart (1 Samuel 16:1–7).

Samuel anointed Saul to be the first king of Israel. Although Saul was taller and more handsome than anyone else, his disobedience brought rejection from God and grief to Samuel. When God sent Samuel to anoint a new king from the sons of Jesse, Samuel was swayed by physical appearance and assumed Eliab was God's choice. Because God is the only One who can see the heart of man, God knew Eliab's heart was not right. God also knew David's heart was right; thus, David was chosen to be king.

In verse 7, "outward appearance" is referring to Eliab's countenance and height, not to his clothing. Clothing is not mentioned in the passage. When a woman refers to this verse by saying, "God doesn't look at my outward appearance; He just sees my heart," she has interpreted the verse to mean that God overlooks her clothes. Because God is all-knowing, He is aware of a woman's clothing, not just the condition of her heart.

Even though God is primarily concerned about the heart, a woman should not assume that her clothing is unimportant to Him. How a woman dresses is important to God, for in 1 Timothy 2:9, God commands women to dress modestly. Modest apparel also helps the man avoid the sin of lust that Jesus warned about in Matthew 5:28: "But I say unto you, That whosoever looketh on a woman to lust after her hath committed adultery with her already in his heart."

Investigation

What is meant by "outward appearance" in 1 Samuel 16:7?

_____

_____

_____

_____

How should a woman answer someone who believes the immodest clothes she wears does not matter to God?

_____

_____

_____

_____

In Conclusion

Clothing can be a mirror of the heart.

Guarding the heart is of prime importance
because the heart affects all of life.

Is Thy Heart Right with God?

Have thine affections been nailed to the cross?
Is thy heart right with God?
Dost thou count all things for Jesus but loss?
Is thy heart right with God?

Refrain:

Is thy heart right with God?
Washed in the crimson flood,
Cleansed and made holy, humble and lowly,
Right in the sight of God?

Hast thou dominion o'er self and o'er sin?
Is thy heart right with God?
Over all evil without and within?
Is thy heart right with God?

Are all thy pow'rs under Jesus' control?
Is thy heart right with God?
Does He each moment abide in thy soul?
Is thy heart right with God?

— Elisha A. Hoffman

LESSON 4

Is Legalism Legal?
Part 1

Introduction

What does the word *legalism* mean?

Illustration

Jennifer was extremely proud of her perfect church attendance. Because she believed salvation depended upon good works, she participated in as many ministries and activities as possible. Whenever a worker was needed, she was always quick to volunteer.

One week when Jennifer was assisting in the church nursery, she met a single mother struggling with three small children. Assuming she would appreciate some help, Jennifer gladly offered free babysitting on Saturday afternoons to allow the mother to go grocery shopping or make a trip to the mall. When the pastor announced that an elderly widow was no longer able to drive to church, Jennifer made a special effort to provide a ride for her. She desired to show sympathy and compassion to others, so instead of mingling with her friends,

Jennifer chose to befriend a grieving grandmother who had recently lost her granddaughter due to cancer.

People noticed her kind, thoughtful deeds and praised her. Jennifer was proud of her accomplishments and was confident that a loving God would reward her by allowing her into Heaven.

Was Jennifer guilty of legalism?

Instruction

One form of legalism occurs when a person attempts to earn salvation by performing good works. A woman who depends upon good works will tend to focus on her actions and not consider the condition of her heart. She believes that the quantity and quality of her good works will be the factors that determine her acceptance with God. If she feels confident that her good works are sufficient, she will tend to become proud. If she fears her good works are insufficient, she could be driven to perform even more. By depending upon her own effort to live the Christian life, she will fail to receive what Christ has already done for her on the cross.

Galatians 2:16 explains, "Knowing that a man is not justified by the works of the law, but by the faith of Jesus Christ, even we have believed in Jesus Christ, that we might be justified by the faith of Christ, and not by the works of the law: for by the works of the law shall no flesh be justified." Justification, a one-time act of God toward a guilty sinner, declares the person forgiven and righteous forever in the sight of God. When a woman repents, confesses her sin, and accepts the atoning work of Christ's shed blood on the cross to pay the penalty for her sin, God forgives and justifies her. After a woman is justified, her faith should result in *good works*—the *evidence* of justification and not the *cause* for justification because no amount of good works can ever save anyone from sin. This truth is expressed in the hymn "Rock of Ages, Cleft for Me" by Augustus M. Toplady.

Not the labors of my hands

Can fulfill Thy law's demands;

Could my zeal no respite know,

Could my tears forever flow,

All for sin could not atone;

Thou must save and Thou alone.

Nothing in my hand I bring,

Simply to Thy cross I cling;

Naked, come to Thee for dress,

Helpless, look to Thee for grace;

Foul, I to the fountain fly,

Wash me, Savior, or I die!

Insights

Legalism characterizes the practices of a religious group known as the Pharisees. The Pharisees lived in Jesus' day and were members of a Jewish sect who were notorious for their strict observance of 613 written laws. Jesus did not condemn the Pharisees for their zeal and desire to keep the laws. He condemned them for trusting in their outward performance to gain acceptance with God.

Furthermore, the Pharisees were hypocrites because they kept the laws externally, but their hearts were far from God. Jesus exposed them when He said, "*Ye* hypocrites, well did Esaias prophesy of you, saying, This people draweth nigh unto me with their mouth, and honoureth me with *their* lips; but their heart is far from me. But in vain they do worship me, teaching *for* doctrines the commandments of men" (Matthew 15:7–9). True worship is not the adherence to the external traditions of men; true worship is a sweet-smelling fragrance that comes from a heart that truly loves God and a life that is totally surrendered to Him.

God gives priority to the condition of the heart. Like the Pharisee, a woman can perform good works but not be in a right relationship with God. She may be convinced that because her actions are right, her heart is right. Proverbs 21:2 is a reminder that "Every way of a man *is* right in his own eyes: but the LORD pondereth the hearts." God sees the motives of the heart, and He always desires that a woman's actions flow from a heart that truly loves Him.

Investigation

If a woman depends upon good works for salvation, can she ever be sure she has done enough? Why, or why not?

_____

_____

_____

In Conclusion

Legalism is the attempt to earn salvation by good works.

> *Good works*—the *evidence* of justification
> and not the *cause* for justification

Illustration

Becky desired to grow in her Christian life, so when she heard about a seminar for new believers, she registered right away. In the sessions, Becky took very detailed notes as she listened intently to each speaker. At the close of the seminar, Becky stared at her filled notebook. Even though she was overwhelmed by the substantial amount of new information, she made a commitment to adhere to the disciplines to the best of her ability.

When Becky arrived home, she compiled a lengthy list of rules to follow. Each morning, Becky reviewed the goals to be accomplished, and each evening, she evaluated her performance. She believed the better she could adhere to the list, the more she would grow as a Christian.

Was Becky guilty of legalism?

Instruction

The process of spiritual growth whereby a Christian grows into spiritual maturity is called sanctification. This process is not achieved by the strict adherence to a set of rules. Sanctification takes place as a woman yields herself to the Potter's hands to be molded into His image.

Sanctification involves separation from sin to live a life of holiness. As a woman denies her flesh, the fruit of the Spirit, which is love, joy, peace, longsuffering, gentleness, goodness, faith, meekness, and self-control, will become evident in her life.

Sanctification should affect all areas of a woman's life as she obeys the Word of God through the power of the Holy Spirit. This process continues throughout her lifetime. "Being confident of this very thing, that he which hath begun a good work in you will perform *it* until the day of Jesus Christ" (Philippians 1:6).

Insights

The Christians in the region of Galatia had been influenced by false teachers who taught that, along with a faith in Christ, obedience to the Law of Moses was necessary for justification. Paul found it inconceivable that the believers, who had been freed from the Law when they embraced the gospel by faith and received the Holy Spirit, would continue to observe the Jewish laws and customs to perfect their faith.

> O foolish Galatians, who hath bewitched you, that ye should not obey the truth, before whose eyes Jesus Christ hath been evidently set forth, crucified among you? Are ye so foolish? Having begun in the Spirit, are ye now made perfect by the flesh? (Galatians 3:1, 3).

Paul challenged the believers to depend upon Christ alone as the source for their faith. Paul reminded them that since they had been saved by grace through faith in Christ alone, they should continue to live by grace through faith in Christ alone.

The Christian life is not a list of rules; the Christian life is a personal relationship with Christ. Likewise, Christian growth is not dependent upon the strict adherence to rules; Christian growth is dependent upon the transformation of the attitudes and desires of the heart.

Investigation

Why would a woman choose the difficult task of following a set of rules to live the Christian life?

_____

_____

_____

How were the Galatians deceived after salvation? What truth did Paul give them?

_____

_____

_____

In Conclusion

Legalism is depending upon the strict adherence to rules and standards for spiritual growth and maturity.

> The Christian life is not a list of rules; the Christian life is a personal relationship with Christ.

Illustration

Linda relocated from the noisy, urban area where she had lived for many years to a quiet, rural location. As she cautiously drove the winding roads to familiarize herself with the area, she spotted a quaint, little church nestled peacefully in the picturesque hills. Remembering her former church where the people were distant and cold, she was certain a smaller congregation would be friendly and outgoing. Since the church was only a few miles from her home, she decided to visit.

When Sunday morning arrived, Linda chose her favorite dress and carefully curled her hair. Before leaving the house, she glanced in the mirror one more time to check her appearance.

Linda was unaware that the charter members of the church had formed definite opinions about the way a woman should look.

Anticipating a warm welcome as she entered the church, Linda was startled as one of the older women named Gladys grabbed her arm and pulled her aside.

"My dear, don't you realize curls are worldly?" chided Gladys. "Christians are to have plain, simple hairstyles."

Linda was stunned. She felt embarrassed as Gladys' glaring eyes began to scrutinize her dress.

"Just look at your dress!" scolded Gladys. "The hemline should be at least two inches below the knee. That's what we expect around here."

Linda was so deeply hurt by the comments that she rushed to her car and quickly drove away.

Was Glady being legalistic?

Instruction

When a woman adopts a specific standard, she often expects other women to agree with her. If they do not, she may find it difficult to accept their different opinions since she believes her practice is correct. As a consequence, she may apply pressure to convince others to conform to her standard, or she may impose guilt upon them for disagreeing with her. Both methods could influence others to comply outwardly to her standard even though they do not share the same conviction.

In the previous illustration, Gladys used pressure to try to persuade Linda to abide by her rules. Her rules were her own personal preferences and opinions and were not in the Bible. Since the rules were unbiblical, Gladys should not have tried to force Linda to comply with them when Linda did not have the same convictions.

Insights

The Pharisees attempted to use the method of imposing guilt by accusing Jesus of breaking the Law. Of course, Jesus did not break the

Law; He only broke the Pharisees' misinterpretation of the Law. Not only had the Pharisees formulated hundreds of elaborate but petty rules to interpret the Law, but they had also elevated those rules to be equal to the Law.

To have a personal preference is not wrong as long as the action does not conflict with biblical principles. However, a woman can become like a Pharisee if she allows her personal preferences to become as important as Scripture. Since she is convinced that her standard pleases the Lord, she can be prone to communicate a spirit of pride and spiritual superiority, whether intentional or unintentional. A woman must remember that she will answer to God for herself and not for others.

Investigation

Name examples of human preferences that people elevate to the level of biblical absolutes.

_____

_____

_____

_____

How can a woman convey a spirit of superiority?

_____

_____

_____

_____

How should a woman respond to someone who challenges her about a standard that is unbiblical?

_____

_____

_____

In Conclusion

Legalism elevates personal standards and preferences to the level of biblical absolutes.

A woman must remember that she will answer

to God for herself and not for others.

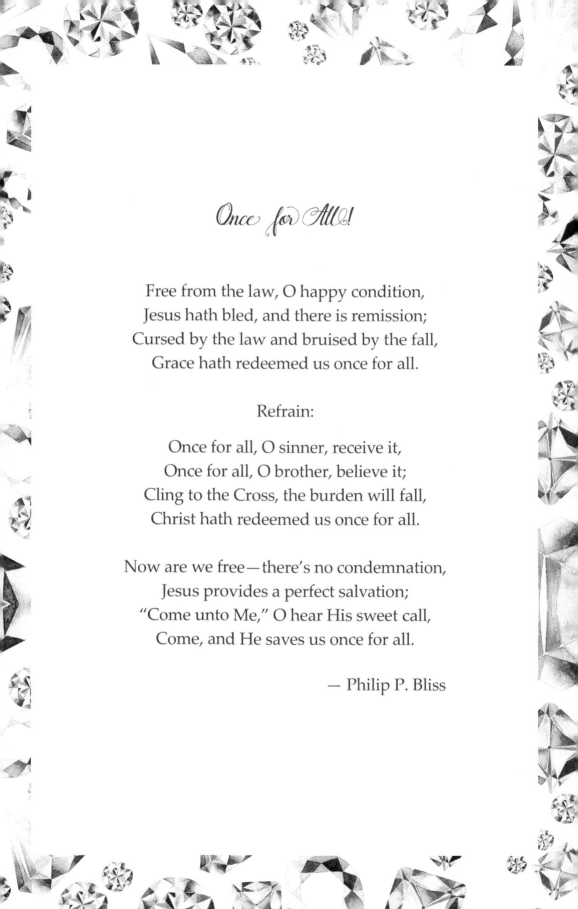

Once for All!

Free from the law, O happy condition,
Jesus hath bled, and there is remission;
Cursed by the law and bruised by the fall,
Grace hath redeemed us once for all.

Refrain:

Once for all, O sinner, receive it,
Once for all, O brother, believe it;
Cling to the Cross, the burden will fall,
Christ hath redeemed us once for all.

Now are we free—there's no condemnation,
Jesus provides a perfect salvation;
"Come unto Me," O hear His sweet call,
Come, and He saves us once for all.

— Philip P. Bliss

LESSON 5

Is Legalism Legal?

Part 2

Introduction

Why are people falsely accused of legalism?

Illustration

Cindy Smith had professed salvation as a child. Now that she had entered her teenage years, her parents were becoming deeply concerned about the immodest clothes she was liking and even beginning to buy. Though she dreaded the confrontation, Mrs. Smith decided to approach Cindy about the matter. After praying about talking to her daughter, she hesitantly knocked on Cindy's door. When Cindy said, "Come in," Mrs. Smith decided to confront her daughter and not sidestep the issue.

"Cindy, your dad and I are bothered about the type of clothes you are choosing to wear. We love you, and because we love you, we would like for you to follow these guidelines as long as you live in our house."

In spite of her daughter's less than agreeable attitude, Mrs. Smith shared the guidelines she and Cindy's dad had prayerfully drafted.

"Rules, rules, rules," griped Cindy as her mother finally left the room. "I'll show them!"

Intent on proving her parents wrong, Cindy decided to search her Bible for the rules they had written. Just as she had suspected, the rules could not be found. Anger welled up within her.

"Legalism!" she yelled as she stormed out of the house with the paper wadded up in her fist. Cindy headed straight to her friends' house to consult with them.

"Oh, c'mon, Cindy, these rules are ridiculous!" criticized one friend as she attempted to read the wrinkled paper. "Your parents are just too strict."

"Yeah, besides, you're old enough to make up your own mind, Cindy. We've decided around here that grace gives us the freedom to do whatever we want. That's our opinion," another friend remarked defiantly.

Cindy wholeheartedly agreed with her friends' comments. *They understand exactly how I feel,* she thought. Eager to escape her parents' outrageous rules, she applied for a job at a local department store. She scrimped and saved money from her meager salary to purchase an inexpensive, used car so she could move in with her friends. Without any rules to follow, Cindy was convinced she was experiencing true freedom.

Was Cindy experiencing true freedom?

Insights

Grace is not a license to sin. Paul makes this point in Romans 6:1 by asking, "What shall we say then? Shall we continue in sin, that grace may abound?" In verse 2, he answers, "God forbid. How shall we, that are dead to sin, live any longer therein?" *God forbid* can be translated "by no means" or "may it never be." Paul was emphatic about not abusing grace. Grace gives a person the power to resist temptation and to do what is right; therefore, God never intended for grace to be an excuse to sin.

Instruction

Life is full of rules not specifically listed in the Bible. To name a few, there are rules for driving, rules at work, rules at school, and rules in sports. Many rules for the routine activities of life are not found in the Bible, but the command for children to obey their parents is clearly given in Ephesians 6:1, which states, "Children, obey your parents in the Lord: for this is right."

God has ordained parents to be in authority, and He has given them the responsibility of implementing biblical principles by making rules and setting standards for their children. Certainly, any rule or standard they make should be for the benefit of the children—not for their harm. Parents should be faithful in their duties because someday they will give an account for how they have fulfilled their responsibilities.

Cindy's parents loved her and desired the best for her. What did they do wrong? When a teenager's heart is not right with the Lord, she is likely to interpret rules and biblical commands as legalism. Because she is rebellious, she seeks freedom from the rules, and the pendulum often swings to the opposite extreme. The opposite extreme involves rejecting her God-given authority by establishing her own lifestyle or by following the ungodly lifestyle of her friends or acquaintances. She considers freedom to be the removal of any unwanted restraints from her life.

True freedom is not experienced by escaping rules; true freedom is experienced by obeying rules with a right heart attitude. Rules set important boundaries that not only protect a person from serious physical injury but also protect a person from a sinful lifestyle that has damaging consequences. Obeying rules allows a person to live a life that pleases the Lord.

Mr. and Mrs. Smith gave Cindy guidelines to teach her what was right, but instituting rules alone will not change the heart of a teenager. If Cindy had chosen to submit to her parents rather than listen to her friends, God could have worked in her life to help her obey the rules with a right heart attitude.

Investigation

Was Cindy right in resisting her parents' rules and charging them with legalism? Why, or why not?

Did Cindy find true freedom when she dressed immodestly? Why, or why not?

How can you explain to young people that establishing their own lifestyle or following the ungodly lifestyle of their friends is not true freedom?

In Conclusion

Freedom is not experienced by rejecting rules. Freedom is experienced by obeying rules with a right heart attitude.

> God never intended for grace to be an excuse to sin.

Illustration

Melissa went forward after an evangelistic message at church. Seeing her response, Mrs. Jones offered to disciple her since her parents were not Christians. Melissa was so touched by Mrs. Jones's genuine love and concern that she gladly accepted her offer.

Melissa loved studying the Bible with Mrs. Jones because they talked about various aspects of the Christian life. One week as they were studying about modesty, Melissa became convicted about her immodest clothes.

"Mrs. Jones, I would like to buy different clothes, but I don't even know where to shop," sighed Melissa.

"Melissa, I will be glad to pick you up and go with you," offered Mrs. Jones.

The two went shopping at the mall the next morning and had a delightful time together. Melissa was pleased to find five suitable outfits.

On Monday morning, Melissa wore one of her new outfits to school. The gang with whom Melissa used to associate noticed right away.

One of the girls sneered and called out, "Hey, Melissa, what's up with the clothes? Is that crazy religion rubbing off on you?"

The jeering remarks of the gang echoed down the long hallway.

"Can you believe it? Melissa has become a *legalist*," another girl scoffed.

Was Melissa a legalist?

Instruction

When a woman lovingly obeys God's instruction to be modest with a desire to please the Lord, she is not a legalist.

When a woman voluntarily submits to the lordship of Christ and dresses as He desires, she is not a legalist.

When a woman willingly chooses to dress according to the biblical principles in the Bible, she is not a legalist.

If a woman is wearing modest clothing, is she legalistic? Only God knows for sure, for He is the only One who can see and know the motives and desires of her heart.

In Conclusion

A woman's heart attitude determines whether or not she is legalistic.

> Only God knows the motives
> and desires of the heart.

May the Mind of Christ, My Savior

May the mind of Christ, my Savior,
Live in me from day to day,
By His love and pow'r controlling
All I do and say.

May the Word of God dwell richly
In my heart from hour to hour,
So that all may see I triumph
Only through His pow'r.

May the love of Jesus fill me,
As the waters fill the sea;
Him exalting, self-abasing—
This is victory.

— Kate B. Wilkinson

LESSON 6

BLURRED VISION

Introduction

What is your view of God?

Illustration

The aroma of freshly baked chocolate chip cookies permeated the air at the ladies' luncheon. As the ladies anxiously waited, the hostess artistically arranged the cookies on the serving tray. Although she used caution in handling the warm cookies, one broke. As the tray was passed around, each lady chose a cookie. When the tray reached the last lady, only the broken pieces were left. The other ladies had taken a whole cookie for themselves not thinking about who would get the broken one.

Instruction

The story in Genesis 13:1–18 talks about Lot whose choice to have the best land eventually brought physical, moral, and spiritual harm to his family. Abraham and Lot were both extremely rich in herds and cattle; therefore, the land was not big enough for them to dwell together. Eventually, tension developed between their herdsmen. Since Abraham wanted to avoid strife, he gave Lot first choice of the land before them. If Lot wanted to go to the left, Abraham would go to the right. If Lot wanted to go to the right, Abraham would go to the left. Abraham and Lot had been in Egypt where Lot had probably acquired a taste for the sinful lifestyle of the world. Perhaps that is why he selfishly chose the well-watered plains of Jordan toward Sodom, a city known for its exceeding sinfulness.

Some valuable lessons can be learned from Lot's life. First, he was selfish in choosing the best land. Next, he was oblivious to the destruction that would come to his family by not separating from sin. Finally, the decisions he made hindered his fellowship with God.

When a woman's fellowship with God is hindered, she will experience a condition called *blurred vision,* which results in a wrong view of God. Having a right view of God is important in understanding modesty because only God has the authority to define modesty. When God is viewed as a tyrant, modesty will most likely be perceived as a ridiculous list of legalistic rules aimed at restricting freedom. If God is viewed solely as a God of love, modesty will probably be regarded as an option, assuming God will overlook whatever offends Him.

When a woman allows her mind to define modesty, her thoughts can be distorted because of selfish desires. If she depends upon the world to define modesty, her values will be tainted by ungodliness and vain philosophies. To have a right view of modesty, a woman needs to understand the character of God and His authority over her life. By studying God's holiness and lordship, insights can be gained on how each one relates to modesty.

Investigation

How can a woman discern if she has blurred vision?

_____

_____

How does blurred vision produce a wrong view of modesty?

_____

_____

_____

HOLINESS

God's holiness is His magnificent and transcendent character that sets Him apart from His creation. The prophet Isaiah declared, "For thus saith the high and lofty One that inhabiteth eternity, whose name *is* Holy; I dwell in the high and holy *place*" (Isaiah 57:15a).

God is distinctly different, separate, and unique. The term "wholly other" is used in biblical theology to describe the vast difference between God and everything else. His holiness goes far beyond the power of thought to fully grasp and comprehend, and no human language can completely express or describe His holiness.

God is perfect without even a trace of sin, impurity, or imperfection of any kind. God is the only One who is perfect in holiness; therefore, He is the only standard for holiness.

Instruction

When the prophet Isaiah encountered the holiness of God, he cried, "...Woe *is* me! For I am undone; because I *am* a man of unclean lips, and I dwell in the midst of a people of unclean lips: for mine eyes have seen the King, the LORD of hosts" (Isaiah 6:5). Contemplating God's holiness helps a person realize the seriousness of sin. Sin is more than bad habits, evil thoughts, and unkind words; the root cause of sin is a heart condition whereby a person rebels against the authority of God and chooses to live life his own way.

First Peter 1:15–16 commands, "But as he which hath called you is holy, so be ye holy in all manner of conversation [conduct]; Because it is written, Be ye holy; for I am holy." A Christian is set apart by God's grace for God's purposes. Between salvation and glorification in Heaven, a Christian is called to a life of personal holiness. Holiness requires separation from sin and the pursuit of righteousness. Because holiness includes moral purity, a person's appearance should reflect moral purity and decency. Since holiness involves separation from sin and the world, a person's appearance should indicate separation from sin and the world. As a person becomes holy, modesty should be the natural result.

In their book, *The Beauty of Modesty*, David and Diane Vaughan present modesty in this intriguing way: "In teaching holiness, we will be restoring modesty, for holiness is its soil."[1] The thought that holiness is the soil from which modesty grows is enlightening. In planting a vegetable garden, fertile soil is required for the plants to grow properly and produce abundant crops. The same is true for modesty. Modesty needs the fertile soil of holiness and godly character to result in a godly appearance.

A lesson using soil is found in Matthew 13:1–23. The parable of the four soils represents man's receptivity to the Word of God, but the parable can be used to illustrate a woman's receptivity to instruction regarding modesty. The hard soil can illustrate the woman's heart that hears instruction but scorns and refutes the idea, giving absolutely no consideration to the matter. The rocky soil can illustrate the woman's heart that receives the instruction but soon disregards the truth to avoid criticism and rejection. The thorny soil can illustrate the woman's heart that receives the instruction but is soon lured by the enticements of the world. The good soil can illustrate the woman's heart that receives the instruction and then responds by adopting strong convictions in her heart. These convictions do not change despite criticism, rejection, or the attractions of the world.

Investigation

What characteristics of a woman indicate that her heart is like good soil?

What characteristics of a woman indicate that her heart is like bad soil?

LORDSHIP

An earthly lord has authority, power, and control over other people. The lordship of Christ ascribes to Him supreme power and rule over the entire universe. The child of God who submits to the lordship of Christ denies selfish desires and surrenders daily to Christ's will.

Instruction

THE LORDSHIP OF CHRIST
NECESSITATES REPENTANCE.

Before Christ can be Lord in a woman's life, genuine repentance needs to take place. Repentance is more than simply saying, "I'm sorry." Repentance involves a change of mind and heart that produces a changed life. A woman who is repentant not only has a desire to be free from the penalty of sin but also has a desire to be free from the power of sin.

THE LORDSHIP OF CHRIST IMPLIES OWNERSHIP.

The Christian woman has been bought with a price, the precious blood of Jesus Christ. "What? Know ye not that your body is the temple of the Holy Ghost *which is* in you, which ye have of God, and ye are not your own? For ye are bought with a price: therefore glorify God in your body, and in your spirit, which are God's" (1 Corinthians 6:19–20).

THE LORDSHIP OF CHRIST REQUIRES SUBMISSION.

Christ will not force a woman to submit; He is not a demanding tyrant. He longs to have a woman's submission, but a woman must willingly choose to yield to Christ and allow Him to be Lord of her life. The blessing she experiences is an intimate fellowship with the Lord.

THE LORDSHIP OF CHRIST EXPECTS OBEDIENCE.

Jesus asked, "And why call ye me, Lord, Lord, and do not the things which I say?" (Luke 6:46). If a woman acknowledges Jesus as Lord but does not obey Him, she is a hypocrite. Whenever she hears God's Word, she should gladly obey Him from a heart of love. "But be ye doers of the word, and not hearers only, deceiving your own selves" (James 1:22).

THE LORDSHIP OF CHRIST
IS A CALL TO DISCIPLESHIP.

A woman who is a disciple follows Christ by learning and adhering to the doctrines and teachings in the Bible. As she studies the Word of God, the Holy Spirit gives her the ability to comprehend God's priorities and purposes for her life. When she walks in obedience to the truth she has learned, she will experience a close oneness and fellowship with Christ.

THE LORDSHIP OF CHRIST
DEMANDS A COST.

A woman who becomes like Christ can expect to receive the treatment Christ received. Jesus warned, "If the world hate you, ye know that it hated me before *it hated* you. If ye were of the world, the world would love his own: but because ye are not of the world, but I have chosen you out of the world, therefore the world hateth you" (John 15:18–19).

Rejection is extremely difficult to endure. Women naturally have a desire to be loved and accepted. When faced with the decision whether to obey Christ or to fit in with the crowd, Christ expects His disciples to obey Him. This is why Jesus gives the warning to count the cost before making a commitment.

THE LORDSHIP OF CHRIST
GIVES MEANING AND PURPOSE TO LIFE.

Knowing Christ as Lord brings true joy. David, the well-known psalmist, wrote, "Thou wilt shew me the path of life: in thy presence *is* fulness of joy; at thy right hand *there are* pleasures for evermore" (Psalm 16:11). The greatest joy comes from delighting in the One who loves you the most, and Christ's love far surpasses any other.

The lordship of Christ gives meaning and purpose to life because God's plans are always best. Jeremiah 29:11 promises, "For I know the thoughts that I think toward you, saith the LORD, thoughts of peace, and not of evil, to give you an expected end." Even if the present circumstances are difficult and His purpose impossible to understand, God is always good, and His way is always best.

Insights

"I beseech you therefore, brethren, by the mercies of God, that ye present your bodies a living sacrifice, holy, acceptable unto God, *which is* your reasonable service" (Romans 12:1). When Paul used the word *beseech*, he was not making a casual request. He was fervently begging the Christians to fully embrace their new life in Christ. His ultimate desire was for them to live a life totally dedicated to God and to His service.

The basis for this life of service is the wonderful mercies of God. Because of His great mercy, living a life totally dedicated to God is the only reasonable or logical response for the believer, and God is perfectly right in expecting such a response.

A sacrifice in the Old Testament involved the killing of an animal that was to be burned on the altar in the tabernacle courtyard. The sacrifice was considered complete because the death of the animal was required. Similarly, a woman must yield her life in full surrender to God on His altar and allow Him to break any existing bondages to the things of the world. Only then will the sacrifice be full, complete, and acceptable to God.

The phrase "living sacrifice" sounds like a contradiction but is not. Once a person has fully surrendered to Christ, they are raised up to a new life of dedication, devotion, and service to Him, empowered by the Holy Spirit and not their flesh. Paul explained this truth when he said, "I am crucified with Christ: nevertheless I live; yet not I, but Christ liveth in me: and the life which I now live in the flesh I live by the faith of the Son of God, who loved me, and gave himself for me" (Galatians 2:20).

The lordship of Christ means He has supreme authority over a Christian woman, and she can no longer say, "It's *my* body, and I can treat it however I want." The lordship of Christ means He has supreme authority over her decisions, and she can no longer say, "It's *my* life, and I can do whatever I want." The lordship of Christ means He has supreme authority over her clothes, and she can no longer say, "It's *my* choice, and I can wear whatever I want." The lordship of Christ means she can no longer say, "*My* will, not Thine, Lord." Lordship can be summarized with this convicting statement: "You can say 'No,' and you can say 'Lord,' but you cannot say 'No, Lord.'"[2] If Christ is truly Lord, the only answer that can be given is "Yes, Lord."

Investigation

What does the lordship of Christ mean?

_____

_____

_____

Judges 21:25 says, "In those days *there was* no king in Israel: every man did *that which was* right in his own eyes." Can a Christian woman become like Christ if she insists on doing what is right in her own eyes? Explain.

_____

_____

_____

_____

In what specific ways can a Christian woman demonstrate that Christ is Lord in her life?

_____

_____

_____

_____

In Conclusion

A right view of God's holiness and lordship should affect modesty.

> "You can say 'No,' and you can say 'Lord,'
>
> but you cannot say 'No, Lord.'"

I Surrender All

All to Jesus I surrender,
All to Him I freely give;
I will ever love and trust Him,
In His presence daily live.

Refrain:

I surrender all, I surrender all;
All to Thee, my blessed Savior,
I surrender all.

All to Jesus I surrender,
Humbly at His feet I bow,
Worldly pleasures all forsaken,
Take me, Jesus, take me now.

All to Jesus I surrender,
Lord, I give myself to Thee;
Fill me with Thy love and power,
Let Thy blessings fall on me.

— Judson W. Van DeVenter

LESSON 7

The Immoral Woman

Introduction

What causes a woman to become immoral?

Illustration

Marilyn and Sophia lived in the same neighborhood. They spent many hours playing together at the park on Saturday afternoons, and because they were in the same grade at school, they helped each other with homework assignments in the evenings. Their lives were quite similar except for their relationships with their fathers.

Marilyn's father spent time with her and expressed his love in numerous ways. He complimented her on her achievements and encouraged her when she was depressed. Whenever she wanted to share her thoughts or discuss her problems, he always set aside the time to listen.

Sophia's father was usually too busy with his work and favorite hobbies to spend time with her. When she tried to please him, he often responded by asking, "Is that the best you can do?" Sophia never had an opportunity to have a personal talk with her father. As a result, she felt rejected and unloved.

As Marilyn and Sophia became teenagers, they developed different interests and spent less time together. Marilyn became involved in the local church where she developed several close friendships. Sophia spent most of her time alone. To find love and acceptance, she dressed immodestly and flirted with guys who were immoral in hopes of winning their approval.

A few years later, Marilyn married a wonderful man who was attracted to her godly character. Unfortunately, Sophia had not found a marriage partner. Despite the fact that she was flirtatious and wore provocative clothes to gain the attention of men, all the relationships she experienced resulted in rejection and deep hurt.

Instruction

A daughter who does not receive love and acceptance from her father will be driven to perform in hopes of winning his approval. After many attempts and failures, she will struggle with feelings of rejection and inferiority. Her insatiable desire for acceptance will cause her to flaunt her body around immoral men, which often leads to sin.

Because the relationships she experiences are shallow and short-lived, she will harbor bitterness and anger toward men for not meeting her needs. Consequently, she will experience difficulty as she attempts to relate to any male authority figure in her life.

If she does marry, a satisfying, intimate relationship will be unlikely because of the barriers she has erected. To prevent further hurts, she will be domineering in an attempt to satisfy her needs. Her manipulation and control of her husband will likely drive him away. In desperation, she will resort again to immoral relationships in an effort to find fulfillment and happiness.

Investigation

What factors might contribute to the development of an immoral woman?

FAMILY RELATIONSHIPS

_____

_____

EMOTIONAL

_____

_____

ENVIRONMENTAL

_____

_____

CULTURAL

_____

_____

Why would a woman want to pursue an immoral lifestyle?

_____

_____

_____

Insights

There is forgiveness for anyone entangled in immorality as illustrated in the life of the Samaritan woman in John 4:3–29.

> He [Jesus] left Judaea, and departed again into Galilee. And he must needs go through Samaria. Then cometh he to a city of Samaria, which is called Sychar, near to the parcel of ground that Jacob gave to his son Joseph. Now Jacob's well was there. Jesus therefore, being wearied with *his* journey, sat thus on the well: *and* it was about the sixth hour. There cometh a woman of Samaria to draw water: Jesus saith unto her, Give me to drink (vv. 3–7).

The Jews avoided traveling through Samaria because the Samaritans were "half-breeds" since they had intermarried with the Assyrians and mixed with their idolatrous religion. Jesus, however, purposed to go through Samaria regardless of the cultural restriction because He knew that a woman there would receive the living water He had to offer.

After traveling for several hours on foot, Jesus and His disciples were all tired, hungry, and thirsty. Jesus remained alone at the well while the disciples went into the city to buy food. While He sat and waited for their return, a Samaritan woman came to draw water. Women usually visited the well in the mornings and evenings, but this woman came at noon. Perhaps she was avoiding any encounters with the other women in the town because she was ashamed of her bad reputation and feared being scorned or ridiculed.

Jesus initiated the conversation by asking for a drink. When the woman recognized He was a Jew, she was surprised He spoke to her since the Jews despised the Samaritans. Besides, the custom dictated that a man, especially a rabbi, not speak to a strange woman in public. What was even more amazing was His willingness to touch and drink from her vessel since Jewish custom would have pronounced Him unclean.

Then saith the woman of Samaria unto him, How is it that thou, being a Jew, askest drink of me, which am a woman of Samaria? For the Jews have no dealings with the Samaritans. Jesus answered and said unto her, If thou knewest the gift of God, and who it is that saith to thee, Give me to drink; thou wouldest have asked of him, and he would have given thee living water (vv. 9–10).

Next, Jesus diverted the woman's attention from His physical thirst to her spiritual thirst. The woman failed to understand what Jesus meant by the "living water;" thus, she continued to reason from her human perspective.

The woman saith unto him, Sir, thou hast nothing to draw with, and the well is deep: from whence then hast thou that living water? Art thou greater than our father Jacob, which gave us the well, and drank thereof himself, and his children, and his cattle? Jesus answered and said unto her, Whosoever drinketh of this water shall thirst again: But whosoever drinketh of the water that I shall give him shall never thirst; but the water that I shall give him shall be in him a well of water springing up into everlasting life. The woman saith unto him, Sir, give me this water, that I thirst not, neither come hither to draw (vv. 11–15).

The woman's routine was to make daily trips to the well. She undoubtedly was bewildered when Jesus offered her water to quench her thirst forever. Nevertheless, she requested the water in hopes that her frequent trips to the well carrying the heavy clay vessel would no longer be necessary.

Jesus was aware that the woman did not fully comprehend His words, but before Jesus could give her the living water, He knew she needed to acknowledge her sin. Jesus then proceeded to confront her about her sinful relationships.

Jesus saith unto her, Go, call thy husband, and come hither. The woman answered and said, I have no husband. Jesus said unto her, Thou hast well said, I have no husband: For thou hast had five husbands; and he whom thou now hast is not thy husband: in that saidst thou truly. The woman saith unto him, Sir, I perceive that thou art a prophet (vv. 16–19).

At first, the woman tried to hide her sin by answering, "I have no husband." She did not lie, but neither did she tell the whole truth. Jesus proceeded to go beyond her present situation to divulge all her past relationships. No wonder the woman marveled at the Stranger's knowledge of her. By calling Him a prophet, she was agreeing that the words He had spoken were true. The woman had finally come to the point of confessing who she really was—a sinner.

Since the Samaritans believed their Messiah would come, Jesus told her, "I that speak unto thee am *he*" (v. 26). When she heard these words, she realized He was more than a prophet; He was indeed the long-awaited Messiah.

Anxious to share the news, the woman hurried into the city. When she saw the men, she beckoned, "Come, see a man, which told me all things that ever I did: is not this the Christ?" (v. 29). Why did the woman say that Jesus told her "*all* things that *ever* I did" when He had only confronted her about her relationships with men? Perhaps she was admitting that she had spent her entire life seeking for a relationship to fill the inner void she felt inside. All her failed marriages only testified to her emptiness. When Jesus offered Himself to satisfy her longing, she believed on Him, and her thirst for love was finally satisfied.

God gives us thirst for love,

And then makes bitter all the earthly wells

Wherein we seek to satisfy our burning.

And so we look above,

And find at last the only Spring that quells

The longing and the yearning.[1]

In Conclusion

Christ can satisfy the inner desires of the heart and transform the life of any woman, including an immoral woman.

Only Jesus can satisfy the thirsty soul.

Satisfied

All my lifelong I had panted
For a drink from some cool spring
That I hoped would quench the burning
Of the thirst I felt within.

Refrain:

Hallelujah! I have found Him
Whom my soul so long has craved!
Jesus satisfies my longings;
Thro' His blood I now am saved.

Feeding on the husks around me
Till my strength was almost gone,
Longed my soul for something better,
Only still to hunger on.

Well of water, ever springing,
Bread of life, so rich and free,
Untold wealth that never faileth,
My Redeemer is to me.

— Clara T. Williams

LESSON 8

The Unfaithful Wife

Introduction

Why would a woman be unfaithful to a husband who is faithful to her?

Illustration

Grace met Bob at college during their senior year. They spent a lot of time together between classes, so their relationship developed quickly. Bob was excited because he had never had a sweetheart before, whereas Grace had been deeply involved in previous relationships but did not divulge her secret.

After graduation, they had a simple wedding and settled into a small apartment. Their plan was to wait at least two years to have children until they were financially stable. After six months of marriage, Grace suspected she was pregnant, so she reluctantly made a doctor appointment. When the obstetrician informed her that the ultrasound indicated twins, Grace was stunned.

A couple months after the twins were born, Bob began to work extra hours to cope with the financial pressure. With Bob away from home most of the time, Grace became frustrated with the crying babies, so she decided to apply for a secretarial job.

Grace's boss at the office was a handsome man who was single. They enjoyed each other's company at lunch and shared many common interests. As their conversations became more personal and intimate, their emotions began to escalate. While gazing into her eyes, her boss reached over and tenderly stroked her face and suggested she start making frequent visits to his apartment after work. Grace was ecstatic.

On the evenings when Grace arrived home past the usual time, she gave Bob various excuses for being late. When Bob eventually found out about the affair, he was devastated.

Insights

Proverbs 7 gives an apt description and illustration of an unfaithful wife.

> My son, keep my words, and lay up my commandments with thee. Keep my commandments, and live; and my law as the apple of thine eye. Bind them upon thy fingers, write them upon the table of thine heart. Say unto wisdom, Thou *art* my sister; and call understanding *thy* kinswoman: That they may keep thee from the strange woman, from the stranger *which* flattereth with her words. For at the window of my house I looked through my casement, And beheld among the simple ones, I discerned among the youths, a young man void of understanding, Passing through the street near her corner; and he went the way to her house, In the twilight, in the evening, in the black and dark night: And, behold, there met him a woman *with* the attire of an harlot, and subtil of heart. (She *is* loud and stubborn; her feet abide not in her house: Now *is she* without, now in the streets, and lieth in wait at every corner.) So she caught him, and kissed him, *and* with an impudent face said unto him, *I have* peace offerings with me; this day have I payed my vows. Therefore came I forth to meet thee, diligently to

seek thy face, and I have found thee. I have decked my bed with coverings of tapestry, with carved *works*, with fine linen of Egypt. I have perfumed my bed with myrrh, aloes, and cinnamon. Come, let us take our fill of love until the morning: let us solace ourselves with loves. For the goodman *is* not at home, he is gone a long journey: He hath taken a bag of money with him, *and* will come home at the day appointed. With her much fair speech she caused him to yield, with the flattering of her lips she forced him. He goeth after her straightway, as an ox goeth to the slaughter, or as a fool to the correction of the stocks; Till a dart strike through his liver; as a bird hasteth to the snare, and knoweth not that it *is* for his life. Hearken unto me now therefore, O ye children, and attend to the words of my mouth. Let not thine heart decline to her ways, go not astray in her paths. For she hath cast down many wounded: yea, many strong *men* have been slain by her. Her house *is* the way to hell, going down to the chambers of death (Proverbs 7:1–27).

Instruction

Solomon, a king in Israel, was the wisest man who ever lived. He wrote the book of Proverbs to give wisdom for godly living. Chapter 7 was written to his son, but there are valuable lessons in the passage for women as well.

The scene begins as a young man approaches the corner where an adulterous woman makes herself visible. Because she is "dressed to kill," the man finds the temptation hard to resist. His lack of wisdom makes him an easy target for her attack and leaves him gullible to her forthcoming lies and deception.

The incident happens at night because this woman knows that night is the time to seduce those who might be vulnerable to her enticements. Besides, she sees no reason not to seize the opportunity since her husband is away.

Although the woman is not a harlot, her clothing portrays a harlot, and her heart is sly, cunning, and devious as a harlot. She acts like a harlot by taking to the street to gratify her sexual desires. Her clothes are provocative and give the message, "I am available." She feels no shame as she promises her body but not her heart.

She neglects her responsibilities at home and breaks her commitment to her husband in order to be free to pursue a gullible victim to meet her needs. She does not manifest a meek and quiet spirit but is self-willed, disobedient, stubborn, and rebellious.

The adulterous woman is bold and aggressive as she kisses the man in spite of the fact that he is a stranger. Relationship is not important to her, only sex, and her kiss is just a taste of the sensuality to come.

She has just returned from the temple with leftover meat from her peace offerings, which must be consumed before the end of the day. Her hypocrisy is evident as she pretends to be religious by desiring to keep the ceremonial law while, at the same time, seducing the man to violate God's moral law. She inflates his ego by offering him some of the meat for them to enjoy together. This adulterous woman knows the power of making him feel special; sometimes, that is all that is necessary.

She continues to allure him as she describes her bed as a way of inviting him to the privacy of her house. Her detailed description of a beautiful, perfumed bed is intended to stimulate his imagination, awaken his senses, and inflame his passions as he anticipates the touches, smells, and pleasures he will experience.

This woman is deceptive as she calls their affair *love* instead of lust. The desire for immediate gratification is emphasized without any mention of undesirable consequences. She smooths over the fact that she is an adulterous wife by referring to her husband as the "goodman." Since he is on a long journey, she assures her "lover" they will have plenty of time to relax and enjoy themselves. She provides yet another reason to go ahead since there is no risk of her husband's coming home unexpectedly.

She uses flattery to manipulate the man to yield. Exaggerated praise may boost the ego but it can be destructive to the heart and life. Even if spoken with emotion, flattery is not genuine love because the person is not sincerely interested in the welfare of the other person.

The power of an adulterous woman is seen in the fact that the man goes after her *straightway*, or "immediately," without considering the consequences or cost involved. He is like a man bound in chains, unable to resist the temptation and shame. An analogy is made of an ox who thinks he is on the road to green, lush pastures when he is en route to the slaughterhouse, or of a fool who thinks he is headed for pleasure when he is about to reap severe repercussions. He succumbs to her embrace while he dreams of only satisfaction and contentment. Like an animal so greedy of food that it does not see the trap that is set, he has no idea that his life will end in miseries far greater than his temporary pleasures.

The adulterous woman has not ruined just one man, or even a few men, but many men. They are not just weak men but strong men. They are not merely foolish men but men of great riches, wisdom, and power. The damage is devastating to a man's reputation, character, job, money, marriage, or family. The consequences are immediate and sometimes ongoing, even permanent. The sin can be forgiven, but the memory still lingers.

Proverbs 7:27 warns, "Her house *is* the way to hell, going down to the chambers of death." Proverbs 5:3–5 adds, "For the lips of a strange woman drop *as* an honeycomb, and her mouth *is* smoother than oil: But her end is bitter as wormwood, sharp as a two-edged sword. Her feet go down to death; her steps take hold on hell."

Investigation

What strategies did the woman in Proverbs 7 use to entice the man?

SIGHT

_____

_____

SMELL

_____

_____

TASTE

_____

_____

HEARING (Flattery)

_____

_____

TOUCH

_____

_____

OTHER STRATEGIES

_____

_____

Why would a woman pretend to be spiritual yet pursue immorality?

_____

_____

_____

Define *love* and *lust*. Why does a woman confuse lustful passions with love?

_____

_____

_____

What are some of the consequences when a person pursues immorality?

_____

_____

_____

Many women have succumbed to the advances of an adulterous man. What lessons can you apply from this passage to help you avoid immorality?

_____

_____

_____

Insights

Hosea was a prophet in the Old Testament. He warned the Israelites of God's coming judgment because they were worshiping false gods when they should have been worshiping Jehovah, the one true God. Israel was guilty of committing spiritual adultery since they were breaking the covenant God had made with them.

The book of Hosea tells a painful narrative of Hosea, a faithful husband, and Gomer, his unfaithful wife. God gave Hosea the command to "Go, take unto thee a wife of whoredoms [harlot]" (Hosea 1:2b). The command probably seemed inconceivable to a prophet of God; nevertheless, Hosea obeyed God and married Gomer even though he knew ahead of time she would commit adultery.

After Gomer bore three children, she left Hosea to seek other lovers. During this time, Hosea remained faithful to Gomer in spite of the fact that she was unfaithful to him. Then God instructed Hosea to buy her back and be reconciled to her. "So I bought her to me for fifteen *pieces* of silver, and *for* an homer of barley, and an half homer of barley [perhaps worth fifteen more pieces of silver]" (3:2). This was not an exorbitant price to pay because Gomer had so cheapened herself by her sinful lifestyle that she was only worth thirty pieces of silver—the price of a slave.

The fact that Gomer was unfaithful to Hosea when he was faithful in his love for her is puzzling. One of Satan's strategies is to convince the woman that God has denied her something that would be beneficial. Satan convinced Eve in the Garden of Eden that God was denying them the opportunity to become "as gods, knowing good and evil" (Genesis 3:5). Satan has been breeding discontent in the hearts of women ever since and causing them to covet relationships and possessions that are not in God's will. A woman can resist Satan's lie if she will purpose to be thankful and content with what God has provided. "*Let your* conversation [conduct] *be* without covetousness [greed]; *and be* content with such things as ye have: for he hath said, I will never leave thee, nor forsake thee" (Hebrews 13:5).

Instruction

Hosea's marriage to Gomer was an illustration of God's steadfast covenant with His people. Hosea's continual love for Gomer depicted God's never-ending love for Israel, and Gomer's promiscuous behavior in seeking other lovers represented Israel's adultery in turning to idols. Just as Hosea's heart was broken over his wife's betrayal, God's heart was broken over the Israelites' unfaithfulness.

The book of Hosea can be applied today to show God's desire to restore a wayward believer. Although the believer is joined to Christ, he can commit spiritual adultery by being drawn away by "the lust of the flesh, and the lust of the eyes, and the pride of life" (1 John 2:16b). God's heart is grieved whenever a believer departs into sin, yet God is faithful to forgive if only the believer will repent. "If we confess our sins, he is faithful and just to forgive us *our* sins, and to cleanse us from all unrighteousness" (1 John 1:9).

What amazing love!

Investigation

What heart attitudes cause a Christian woman to commit spiritual adultery?

_____

_____

_____

Why do some women today leave good, loving husbands?

_____

_____

_____

How can a woman learn to be content with what God has provided for her?

_____

_____

_____

In Conclusion

Today's excitement may lead to tomorrow's destruction.

> The adulterer has no idea that his life may end
> in miseries far greater than his temporary pleasures.

Yield Not to Temptation

Yield not to temptation, For yielding is sin.
Each victory will help you Some other to win.
Fight manfully onward; Dark passions subdue.
Look ever to Jesus; He will carry you through.

Refrain:

Ask the Savior to help you
Comfort, strengthen, and keep you.
He is willing to aid you;
He will carry you through.

Shun evil companions; Bad language disdain.
God's name hold in rev'rence, Nor take it in vain.
Be thoughtful and earnest, Kindhearted and true.
Look ever to Jesus; He will carry you through.

To him that o'ercometh God giveth a crown.
Through faith we shall conquer Though often cast down.
He, Who is our Saviour, Our strength will renew.
Look ever to Jesus; He will carry you through.

— Horatio R. Palmer

LESSON 9

Character Clothing

Introduction

How can clothing reveal a woman's character?

Illustration

Teresa volunteered to provide the decorations for the upcoming mother-daughter banquet. Driving around town, she noticed the eye-catching sale sign on the craft store window. Teresa reasoned that this would be the perfect opportunity to search for drastically reduced items, so without hesitation, she decided to stop and browse around.

As she walked from her car to the store, she noticed three girls in front of her. The first girl had on a pair of short shorts and a crop top. The second girl was dressed in a pair of low-rise, distressed jeans and a sheer blouse. The third girl modeled a miniskirt and a tight T-shirt with a suggestive message.

A guy nearby noticed the girls, whistled, and motioned for them to come his way. The girls giggled when they saw his flirtatious smile and quickly climbed into his car. Teresa was deeply concerned as the car drove away.

Instruction

Isaiah 3:16 gives this detailed description of the women of Zion: "Moreover the LORD saith, Because the daughters of Zion are haughty, and walk with stretched forth necks and wanton eyes, walking and mincing *as* they go, and making a tinkling with their feet."

The prophet Isaiah validates that the message is from God by stating, "Moreover the LORD saith." Isaiah established the fact that God was the One who had noticed their appearance and actions, and that He would be the One to bring future judgment upon them.

The "daughters of Zion" were the wives or daughters of rulers, princes, or elders. Their pride was clearly evidenced by their gestures and the ornaments they wore to attract attention.

A haughty person displays an attitude of pride and superiority by despising others who are thought to be inferior. The women's haughtiness was evident as they extended their necks in an arrogant manner to appear stately and tall.

"Wanton" describes a person who is given to self-indulgent flirtation. The women flirted by using immoral glances to stir up lustful desires in men. To be more seductive, the women applied black powder to their eyelids to draw attention to their eyes.

"Mincing" was a special way of walking where women tiptoed in a stiff, formal manner so their heels did not touch the ground. The women wore little bells, chains, or bracelets around their ankles that made a tinkling sound to call attention to themselves.

Insights

The daughters of Zion had become addicted to wealth and fashion. Because they focused more on physical beauty than on their worship of God, Isaiah prophesied God's future judgment upon them. Isaiah warned that God would strip them from the crowns of their heads to the soles of their feet of everything that had brought them pride. The women would be afflicted with a disease that would cause their hair to fall out, and they would walk in nakedness, humiliated and disgraced as captives and slaves. For further punishment, their husbands would be killed. The phrase "her gates shall lament and mourn" is figurative for the deep mourning that would take place because of the destruction of the city.

> Therefore the Lord will smite with a scab the crown of the head of the daughters of Zion, and the LORD will discover their secret parts [make naked]. In that day the Lord will take away the bravery of *their* tinkling ornaments *about their feet*, and *their* cauls [headbands], and *their* round tires [crescent shaped ornaments] like the moon, The chains, and the bracelets, and the mufflers [veils], The bonnets, and the ornaments of the legs, and the headbands, and the tablets, and the earrings, The rings, and nose jewels, The changeable suits of apparel, and the mantles, and the wimples [wrap or veil], and the crisping pins [purses], The glasses [hand mirrors of highly polished metal], and the fine linen, and the hoods, and the veils. And it shall come to pass, *that* instead of sweet smell there shall be stink; and instead of a girdle a rent [a rope]; and instead of well-set hair baldness; and instead of a stomacher [a type of girdle] a girding of sackcloth; *and* burning instead of beauty. Thy men shall fall by the sword, and thy mighty in the war. And her gates shall lament and mourn; and she *being* desolate shall sit upon the ground (Isaiah 3:17–26).

Investigation

How does Isaiah 3:17–26 validate the fact that God sees a woman's appearance?

_____

_____

_____

Insights

Jezebel, one of Israel's queens, is considered to be the most wicked woman in the Bible. Whenever heathen women married men in Israel, they usually brought their idols with them, and Jezebel was no exception. In fact, she was more determined than anyone to have all Israel worship her false gods. To attain her goal, she incited her husband, Ahab, to abandon the worship of Jehovah God and to worship the deities of Baal and Asherah.

In 1 Kings 18:13, this exceptionally forceful woman attempted to kill all the prophets of God, but the lives of a hundred of them were spared because Obadiah, a believer in God, hid them in a cave. Later, she planned to kill Elijah by threatening, "So let the gods do *to me*, and more also, if I make not thy life as the life of one of them by to morrow about this time" (1 Kings 19:2b).

Jezebel was also a domineering woman as clearly seen in the account of Naboth's vineyard. Ahab wanted possession of Naboth's vineyard to have for a garden of herbs since the land was near his house. Ahab offered to give Naboth either a better vineyard or money for the land, but Naboth refused because the land was his God-given inheritance from his fathers. Ahab arrived home depressed, laid down upon his bed, and refused to eat. Jezebel then commanded her husband to "arise, *and* eat bread, and let thine heart be merry: I will give thee the vineyard of Naboth the Jezreelite" (1 Kings 21:7b).

Queen Jezebel wrote letters in her husband's name to the elders of the city and proclaimed a fast. She commanded the elders to bring Naboth before the people along with two witnesses to falsely accuse him of blasphemy against God and the king. After Naboth was stoned to death, Jezebel commanded her husband to go take possession of the vineyard.

The wicked Jezebel was a schemer and a murderer. Sad to say, she never humbled herself but remained proud and egotistical to the end. Right before Jehu came to kill her, "Jezebel heard *of it*; and she painted her face, and tired her head [beautified her hair], and looked out at a window" (2 Kings 9:30b). When most queens would have hidden themselves, Jezebel boldly displayed her stunning appearance to declare her determination to die with dignity as a queen. Outwardly, she died arrayed in all the magnificence of royalty as a Phoenician queen, but inwardly, she died in the same arrogant and shameful way she had lived.

Investigation

Jezebel worshiped the false god Baal. How does who or what a woman worships affect her appearance and actions?

_____

_____

_____

> Physical beauty is abused when it is not combined with godly character.

Insights

King Solomon gives this thought-provoking analogy: "*As* a jewel of gold [ring] in a swine's snout [pig's nose], *so is* a fair [beautiful] woman which is without discretion" (Proverbs 11:22).

A woman with discretion uses discernment and good judgment to recognize and avoid words, actions, and attitudes that could result in undesirable consequences. If a woman lacks discretion, she will be inattentive, indifferent, thoughtless, careless, foolish, and ignorant.

Instruction

Pigs are kept in fenced-in areas. The natural tendency for pigs is to dig with their noses, so to keep them from digging under the fence and escaping, iron rings are put in their noses to cause pain. When they start rooting, the resulting pain discourages their digging.

A beautiful ring in a pig's nose is incongruous. Since a pig's nature is to dig in dirt, mud, and fecal matter, a precious ring smeared with such filth would be detestable. An expensive ring on a woman's finger is attractive, but if the same piece of jewelry were placed in a pig's nose, the sight would be grotesque.

A woman's body is as a jewel of gold if she guards herself from the temptations that bring defilement. But if she lacks discretion, the beauty that was once bestowed upon her becomes a disgrace as she loses her purity. Beauty is abused when it is not combined with modesty.

The natural tendency of a woman who lacks discretion will be to clothe the beautiful body God gave her with immodest clothing. According to Solomon, her beauty will be cheapened like a gold ring in a pig's snout.

Investigation

How does immodesty disgrace a woman's genuine beauty?

_____

_____

_____

Why would a woman want to disgrace the body God has given her?

_____

_____

_____

Why would Solomon use such a detestable example to teach this truth?

_____

_____

_____

In Conclusion

Clothing can reveal a woman's character.

Physical beauty is abused when it is not combined with modesty.

Can Others See Jesus in You?

Christ Jesus has triumphed o'er Satan and death,
And now, praise His name, I am free.
Al-tho' He has gone to the Father's right hand,
Can others see Jesus in me?

O will you give heed to this message tonight,
And to your commission be true?
Are you representing the Savior aright,
Can others see Jesus in you?

The harvest is plenteous, the fields they are white,
Alas! for the lab'rers are few.
'Tis far better not to profess Jesus' name,
If the world cannot see Him in you.

— Leonard C. Voke

Lesson 10

Women of Character

Introduction

What qualities does a woman of good character possess?

Illustration

Elaine was happily married to Steve who pastored a small, rural church. Throughout their ministry, she spent numerous hours comforting hurting women with her compassionate words as well as strengthening younger women by her godly counsel. Whenever the church experienced difficult times, she consistently maintained a steadfast faith that encouraged others. Members of the congregation described her as a humble woman who was loving, kind, and considerate.

Elaine was diligent in managing their modest income so that there would be funds available to donate to visiting missionaries or guest evangelists. She was careful to search for bargains while shopping with the aim of having leftover cash to donate to a worthy charity. Elaine used her money wisely by purchasing only modest clothing, and she encouraged her daughters to do the same.

When the time came for the annual ladies' banquet, everyone stood and clapped in unison when Elaine was highly honored by being presented the Woman of Character Award.

Instruction

Character is measured by the moral qualities a woman possesses. Some character qualities that relate to modesty include deference, discretion, self-control, sensitivity, thriftiness, and virtue. Each quality is important in the choice of appropriate clothing.

Deference can be observed in a woman who possesses a humble and submissive attitude toward others. She voluntarily and cheerfully limits her freedom for the purpose of obeying the judgment, opinion, and will of another person, especially one in authority. She is considerate and respectful in her appearance so as not to be offensive or to cause temptation.

A woman who is guided by discretion uses discernment and good judgment to avoid words, actions, and attitudes that could bring undesirable consequences. In relating to the opposite gender, a woman with discretion avoids inappropriate conversations that could lead to immorality and purposes not to wear provocative clothes that could arouse lust. Her discretion will result in moral purity in all areas of her life.

Self-control is demonstrated when a woman restrains her emotions and actions, especially in difficult situations. Women in general tend to make choices and decisions according to their mood at the time. A woman with self-control will endeavor to refrain herself from making impulsive purchases that are unwise.

Sensitivity gives a person the ability to perceive the needs and emotions of others. Since a woman with sensitivity will be aware of how her appearance provokes the immoral look in a man's eyes, she will avoid the types of clothing that will cause temptation. Her desire will be to edify others by encouraging godliness.

A person who is thrifty manages resources wisely, especially the expenditure of money. A thrifty woman will establish wise priorities to keep from spending money unnecessarily or foolishly. She will experience peace and contentment because she has chosen to use God's resources wisely.

Virtue marks a person with high moral values and principles that have led to godly behavior. A virtuous woman follows a good code of ethics that guide her in making wise, biblical choices.

Some Bible women who are examples of godly character include Abigail, Esther, and Ruth.

Insights

Abigail was a wise woman who was married to Nabal, a foolish man. David and his men had protected Nabal's shepherds and flocks, but Nabal refused to reward them when he had the resources available. David was enraged and, in retaliation, planned to kill Nabal and his men. When Abigail heard the news, she gathered some food as payment for the debt and then set out to make an appeal for David to reconsider his plan.

> And when Abigail saw David, she hasted, and lighted off the ass, and fell before David on her face, and bowed herself to the ground, And fell at his feet, and said, Upon me, my lord, *upon* me *let this* iniquity *be*: and let thine handmaid, I pray thee, speak in thine audience, and hear the words of thine handmaid (1 Samuel 25:23–24).

Because Abigail believed David would someday reign as king, she bowed and acknowledged him as her lord. Abigail explained to David that she had not witnessed the good deed his men performed, so she put all the blame for her husband's bad conduct and foolish actions upon herself. Then she humbly requested, "And now this blessing which thine handmaid hath brought unto my lord, let it even be given unto the young men that follow my lord. I pray thee, forgive the trespass of thine handmaid" (25:27–28a).

After her plea for forgiveness, Abigail wisely redirected David's focus from Nabal to God by reminding him that because he had fought God's battles, God would fight his enemies. Abigail did not desire for David to jeopardize his reputation, endanger his throne, or violate God's will.

> And it shall come to pass, when the Lord [God] shall have done to my lord [David] according to all the good that he hath spoken concerning thee, and shall have appointed thee ruler over Israel; That this shall be no grief unto thee, nor offence of heart unto my lord, either that thou hast shed blood causeless, or that my lord hath avenged himself: but when the Lord shall have dealt well with my lord, then remember thine handmaid. And David said to Abigail, Blessed *be* the Lord God of Israel, which sent thee this day to meet me: And blessed *be* thy advice, and blessed *be* thou, which hast kept me this day from coming to *shed* blood, and from avenging myself with mine own hand…So David received of her hand *that* which she had brought him, and said unto her, Go up in peace to thine house; see, I have hearkened to thy voice, and have accepted thy person (1 Samuel 25:30–33, 35).

Abigail could have condemned David for his desire to kill Nabal, but instead, she wisely advised David to view the situation from God's perspective by allowing God to deal with Nabal. David was wise to give careful attention to Abigail's counsel and to heed her advice.

When Abigail informed her husband what had happened, "his heart died within him, and he became *as* a stone [stroke or heart attack]" (25:37b). About ten days later, Nabal died from God's affliction. When David heard the news, he wasted no time in asking Abigail to become his wife since she was both beautiful and wise.

Investigation

List some of Abigail's character qualities.

_____

_____

_____

_____

Insights

Esther encountered some difficult challenges in her lifetime. She was orphaned as a child and adopted by her cousin Mordecai. When the Jews were exiled from Jerusalem, Mordecai and Esther were taken to Persia. While there, they faced death because Haman, the king's prime minister, wanted to annihilate all the Jews in the Persian Empire. By providential intervention, God arranged for Esther to bring a great deliverance to her people. God is never mentioned in the book of Esther, but His covenant love and care for His people is clearly evident.

When Queen Vashti refused to obey an order from her husband, King Ahasuerus, she was banished, and the search began for a new queen. Esther was taken with other young virgins to the king's house for a year of purification.

> So it came to pass, when the king's commandment and his decree was heard, and when many maidens were gathered together unto Shushan the palace, to the custody of Hegai, that Esther was brought also unto the king's house, to the custody of Hegai, keeper of the women. And the maiden pleased him, and she obtained kindness of him; and he speedily gave her her things for purification, with such things as belonged to her, and seven maidens, *which were* meet to be given her,

out of the king's house: and he preferred her and her
maids unto the best *place* of the house of the women
(Esther 2:8–9).

Even though Hegai was surrounded by many beautiful women,
divine providence prompted him to take special notice of Esther.
As he admired her beauty and character, he concluded that she was
the best candidate to please the king, so he speedily gave Esther her
beauty treatments and seven specifically chosen maidens to assist
her. In addition, Hegai gave Esther and her maidens the largest,
most pleasant room in which to stay.

Each woman would spend one night with the king in his bedroom
unless the king remembered her name and called for her again.
Otherwise, she would live essentially as a widow for the rest of her
life in a luxurious setting under the custody of Shaashgaz, the king's
chamberlain.

When Esther's turn came, she wore only what Hegai recommended.
Apparently, Hegai knew the king's preferences, so he gave her the
very best advice possible. Esther was very wise to accept and follow
that advice.

> So Esther was taken unto king Ahasuerus into his house
> royal in the tenth month, which *is* the month Tebeth,
> in the seventh year of his reign. And the king loved
> Esther above all the women, and she obtained grace and
> favour in his sight more than all the virgins; so that he
> set the royal crown upon her head, and made her queen
> instead of Vashti (Esther 2:16–17).

Haman, the king's prime minister, was furious because Mordecai
refused to bow down to him. Haman bribed King Ahasuerus with
money to be given permission to write a decree to have all the Jews
annihilated. Haman did not know at the time that Queen Esther was
a Jewess.

After the decree went out throughout all the king's provinces,
Mordecai sent a copy to Esther and charged her to approach the king
and make a request for her people. Esther sent word back to Mordecai

warning him that unless the king held out his golden scepter, she would die. Mordecai reminded Esther that she was in serious danger of death regardless of her decision.

Mordecai knew that if Esther did not act, God would deliver His people another way; nevertheless, he appealed to her by asking, "and who knoweth whether thou art come to the kingdom for *such a time as this?*" (4:14c). In response, Esther requested that Mordecai and all the Jews in Shushan not eat or drink for three days and three nights. Esther and her maidens would do the same. Esther realized the seriousness of approaching the king without a summons because such an action was against the law. Her depth of character was evident when she solemnly replied, "and if I perish, I perish" (4:16c).

After Esther had fasted, she put on her royal apparel and courageously stood in the inner court of the king's house. When the king saw her, he held out his golden scepter, and her life was spared. Esther was now in a position where she could be used by God to influence her husband.

At the second banquet that Esther had especially prepared for the king and Haman, Esther pleaded for the king to spare her life and the lives of her people. When Esther informed her husband that Haman was the culprit intending to do this wicked deed, the king rose in wrath and went into the palace garden. In the meantime, Haman was panic-stricken for he knew evil was determined against him.

When the king returned, he found Haman fallen upon Esther's bed, pleading for his life. The king instantly assumed that Haman had evil intentions toward his wife, so to appease his anger and jealously, he ordered for Haman to be hanged.

Esther then appealed to the king to reverse Haman's wicked edict, but since the decree could not be legally revoked, a new mandate was given that allowed the Jews to protect themselves against anyone who would attempt to assault them.

Esther was an orphan, a captive, and a Jew in a pagan nation. Who would have thought she would become the queen who would save an entire nation of people? Only God could arrange such an amazing chain of events. Esther's story gives hope that God can use any woman, no matter how lowly, to be an instrument for His glory if she will trust the invisible hand of God in all of the circumstances of life.

Investigation

What sacrifices did Esther make and what risks did she take to be used by God to bring deliverance to the Jews?

_____

_____

_____

Insights

Due to a severe famine in Israel, Naomi, her husband, and their two sons journeyed to Moab where the oldest son, Mahlon, married Ruth, and Chilion married Orpah, both Moabite women. While in Moab, Naomi's husband and two sons died. Life was difficult for a woman without a husband or sons to provide for her, so when Naomi received the news that the drought had ended in Israel, she decided to return to Bethlehem.

When Naomi started on the journey, she encouraged her two daughters-in-law to go back to their families. Orpah returned, but Ruth forsook her family and pagan homeland and committed herself to following Naomi and her God.

> And Ruth said, Intreat me not to leave thee, *or* to return from following after thee: for whither thou goest, I will go; and where thou lodgest, I will lodge: thy people *shall be* my people, and thy God my God: Where thou diest, will I die, and there will I be buried: the LORD do so to me, and more also, *if ought* but death part thee and me (Ruth 1:16–17).

Ruth and Naomi arrived in Bethlehem during barley harvest. To provide for their physical needs, Ruth volunteered to glean the leftover grain in the fields. By the providence of God, Ruth worked in a field owned by Boaz, a rich relative of Naomi's deceased husband, Elimelech. When Boaz inquired about the foreign woman in his field, a servant informed him of her identity.

Because of Ruth's relationship to Naomi, Boaz accepted responsibility to provide for her needs. He instructed his workers to allow her to glean among the sheaves and to even drop handfuls of grain on purpose for her. Boaz assured Ruth that no one under his authority would taunt her or drive her away from his fields even if she was present before the proper time. If she was thirsty, Boaz allowed her to go to the vessels and drink the water the young men had drawn, and when she was hungry, he permitted her to eat alongside his reapers.

Naomi was mindful of Boaz's generous deeds toward Ruth and, no doubt, pondered them in her heart. Since Naomi desired a husband for Ruth, she knew that Boaz was a promising prospect because he was a relative who could perform the duty of a kinsman-redeemer. The role of a kinsman-redeemer was to marry the widow to provide financial support and to have a son to carry on the family name. When Naomi instructed Ruth to go to Boaz at night, the behavior was not considered immoral because she was acting in accordance with the Jewish custom.

> Wash thyself therefore, and anoint thee, and put thy raiment upon thee, and get thee down to the floor: *but* make not thyself known unto the man, until he shall have done eating and drinking. And it shall be, when he lieth down, that thou shalt mark the place where he shall lie, and thou shalt go in, and uncover his feet, and lay thee down; and he will tell thee what thou shalt do. And she said unto her, All that thou sayest unto me I will do. And she went down unto the floor, and did according to all that her mother in law bade her. And when Boaz had eaten and drunk, and his heart was merry, he went to lie down at the end of the heap of

corn: and she came softly, and uncovered his feet, and laid her down. And it came to pass at midnight, that the man was afraid, and turned himself: and, behold, a woman lay at his feet. And he said, Who *art* thou? And she answered, I *am* Ruth thine handmaid: spread therefore thy skirt over thine handmaid; for thou *art* a near kinsman (Ruth 3:3–9).

When Ruth asked him to "spread therefore thy skirt over thine handmaid," she was requesting Boaz to make a pledge to marry her. In spite of the fact that Boaz was of her father-in-law's generation, Ruth was willing to receive his love, protection, and provision. Boaz, knowing the age span, blessed her for not pursuing after one of the young men. Despite the age difference, Boaz loved Ruth and desired to marry her.

Boaz knew he could not proceed with the marriage until a closer relative was consulted. When that relative declined the offer, Boaz accepted the opportunity to become Ruth's kinsman-redeemer. After the marriage, Ruth became the mother of Obed, which brought her into the genealogy of King David and of the Lord Jesus Christ.

Investigation

What was a *kinsman-redeemer*?

_____

_____

_____

_____

How does Christ fulfill the role of a kinsman-redeemer for the Christian?

_____

_____

_____

_____

In Conclusion

God can use any woman, no matter how lowly, to be an instrument for His glory if she will trust the invisible hand of God in all of the circumstances of life.

> Our character develops in this life
>
> and continues in eternity.

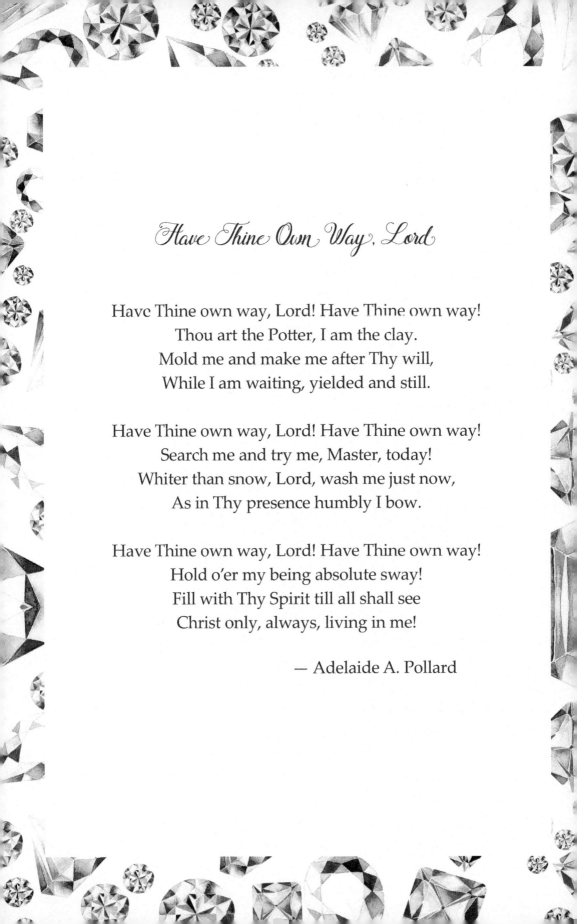

Have Thine Own Way, Lord

Have Thine own way, Lord! Have Thine own way!
Thou art the Potter, I am the clay.
Mold me and make me after Thy will,
While I am waiting, yielded and still.

Have Thine own way, Lord! Have Thine own way!
Search me and try me, Master, today!
Whiter than snow, Lord, wash me just now,
As in Thy presence humbly I bow.

Have Thine own way, Lord! Have Thine own way!
Hold o'er my being absolute sway!
Fill with Thy Spirit till all shall see
Christ only, always, living in me!

— Adelaide A. Pollard

LESSON 11

The Virtuous Woman

Introduction

What are the characteristics of a virtuous woman?

Illustration

Barbara detested housecleaning. Why dust the furniture only to notice more dust the next day? Why vacuum the floors only to detect tracked-in dirt a few hours later? Why clean up the clutter in the house only to repeat the same monotonous task over again?

Barbara was convinced her time was better spent curled up in her favorite chair reading a suspense novel. She often became so engrossed in the plot that she barely noticed when the children came home. Later, when her husband arrived, dinner was not cooked—or even planned. Since enough items could not be found in the almost-empty cupboard, the family had no choice but to eat at a fast-food restaurant.

When her husband left for work in the mornings, Barbara was still asleep because she had stayed up late to connect with all her friends on social media. When she awoke, she usually felt too tired to read a devotional book, so she sluggishly went to the kitchen in hopes that a cup of coffee would motivate her for the day.

Was Barbara a virtuous woman?

Instruction

Proverbs 31:10–31 is an acrostic poem that uses 22 consecutive letters of the Hebrew alphabet to facilitate memorization. The passage is attributed to King Lemuel as taught to him by his mother. Little is known about King Lemuel except that his name means "belonging to God" or "devoted to God."

This poem was read to the woman of the household on Friday evenings at the Jewish Shabbat table as a way to praise her godly qualities and to express gratitude for her hard work. Rather than read the poem as an itemized task list, women should allow the character qualities to inspire them to be their best for God wherever He has placed them.

"Who can find a virtuous woman? for her price *is* far above rubies" (v. 10).

The virtuous woman is governed by godly principles that enable her to control her own life and to manage others. Her great strength of character and moral purity combined with her productive skills qualify her to be a suitable helper for her husband.

This kind of woman is rare and difficult to find, and no number of precious stones can begin to equal her worth. The key to her character is her love and reverence for God, which enhances her value far more than physical beauty or acts of service.

"The heart of her husband doth safely trust in her, so that he shall have no need of spoil" (v. 11).

Her husband has no need to maintain a jealous guard over her since her modest demeanor demonstrates impeccable loyalty to him. Her discretion allows him to be at peace since he can trust her not to disgrace or shame his reputation.

She is frugal and manages the finances so competently that her husband is confident there will always be enough to provide for their needs. There is no reason to seek financial gain or to envy any other man because he is completely content in their relationship.

"She will do him good and not evil all the days of her life" (v. 12).

Her heart is committed to him "for better or for worse, for richer or for poorer, in sickness and in health." His happiness is her constant goal as she meets his needs and even carries out his wishes while he is away. She especially demonstrates her commitment and faithfulness to him by refusing to allow relatives or friends to become rivals.

She has resolved to do him good all the days of his life and all the days of her life as well. If she survives him, she will continue to do him good as she cares for the inheritance.

"She seeketh wool, and flax, and worketh willingly with her hands" (v. 13).

This woman demonstrates her diligence as she searches for raw materials to fashion her own clothes in preference to buying ready-made garments. Designing her own clothes was a way to express her superb skill and exceptional creativity.

Since most women do not weave cloth today, the key word in the verse is "willingly." A woman's work should be done cheerfully with a willing heart to be a good example for her children.

"She is like the merchants' ships; she bringeth her food from afar" (v. 14).

She trades what she has skillfully made to obtain the choicest imported merchandise that is not available locally. Through her wise exchange of commodities, the family's needs are fully met.

"She riseth also while it is yet night, and giveth meat to her household, and a portion to her maidens" (v. 15).

Each morning she sacrifices her own comfort for the benefit of others as she rises before dawn to prepare food for her family and maidens. This decision, made in the warm comfort of her bed, indicates her loving devotion to her family.

The household is run in an orderly manner because daily plans are assigned to each person along with the needed provisions to accomplish the tasks. No one grumbles or complains because everyone is treated fairly.

"She considereth a field, and buyeth it: with the fruit of her hands she planteth a vineyard" (v. 16).

Careful consideration is made before she buys the field to determine if the purchase is at a reasonable price and will be advantageous for her family. Her wisdom and good judgment protect her from making an impulsive, rash decision. When she pays for the field, she uses her own resources to keep from going into debt.

"She girdeth her loins with strength, and strengtheneth her arms" (v. 17).

The Hebrew phrase "she girdeth her loins" was a way to tuck up the traditional long robe worn in Bible times into a girdle or belt. This facilitated movement for activities that required readiness, strength, or endurance.

Because she abhors slothfulness, she vigorously completes her work without hesitation. Her arms become strong as she exercises to bring health and strength to her body. A woman who is a dedicated wife and mother realizes the task is not an easy, comfortable one.

"She perceiveth that her merchandise *is* good: her candle goeth not out by night" (v. 18).

Her high-quality merchandise is always in demand at the marketplace because they are reasonably priced. To learn that her efforts are profitable naturally brings her great satisfaction.

"Her candle [or lamp] goeth not out by night" is not literal but figurative, implying the lamp burns well into the night as she extends her workday. She is resolute in her commitment to her family because she firmly trusts in the promises of God for her daily strength.

"She layeth her hands to the spindle, and her hands hold the distaff" (v. 19).

The spindle and distaff are the most ancient of all the instruments used to make thread and yarn. The spindle was a long, rounded rod with tapered ends used to twist and wind the thread. The distaff held the mass of wool or flax fibers and kept them from becoming tangled during the spinning process.

"She stretcheth out her hand to the poor; yea, she reacheth forth her hands to the needy" (v. 20).

This woman does not spend her wealth exclusively on her family. Instead, she sympathizes with the needs of others and gives liberally to the poor. Her gifts are more than casual donations or convenient acts of charity. They are sacrificial gifts both to her neighbors and to those far away. She experiences the joy that "It is more blessed to give than to receive" (Acts 20:35c).

"She is not afraid of the snow for her household: for all her household *are* clothed with scarlet" (v. 21).

Each member of the household has enough clothes for all seasons of the year. Commentators generally interpret scarlet to mean double garments or double-dyed in the rich-looking scarlet color.

"She maketh herself coverings of tapestry; her clothing *is* silk and purple" (v. 22).

Tapestry is used for beds, pillows, cushions, and furniture. Along with her other skills, she is an interior decorator, and the elegant coverings throughout the house are evidence of God's blessing upon her efforts.

Besides making the house a beautiful place in which to live, she dresses modestly and attractively for her husband. Silk refers to fine white linen that glistened, and the purple dye used for her garments was obtained from the juice of a certain species of shellfish found on the eastern shores of the Mediterranean Sea.

"Her husband is known in the gates, when he sitteth among the elders of the land" (v. 23).

Distinguished men convened at the city gates where they settled business matters, legal issues, and civic questions. Because his wife diligently cares for the household, he is free to give himself to civil interests and gain advancement in the community. A man's good reputation begins with the virtue of his wife.

"She maketh fine linen, and selleth *it*; and delivereth girdles unto the merchant" (v. 24).

Fine linen is not just cloth but a finished garment, indicating this woman is intelligent, ingenious, and industrious.

Girdles are wide sashes or cords worn around the waste by both men and women. After the family is taken care of, she makes girdles to sell and trade to earn additional income for the family.

"Strength and honour *are* her clothing; and she shall rejoice in time to come" (v. 25).

This strength is not physical but of the mind: courage, confidence, and determination. Since *honour* refers to "one who walks with God," her character traits display a woman with divine wisdom who fears the Lord.

Each day she perseveres because she anticipates the imminent benefits and rewards of her labors. She can face the unexpected challenges of the future with confidence because she has made proper preparations. Should difficult times come, her family's needs are satisfied.

"She openeth her mouth with wisdom; and in her tongue *is* the law of kindness" (v. 26).

Her wisdom is evidence that she has developed a right relationship with God who is the source of all wisdom. The insights she has gained allow her to give wise instruction and counsel to her children as she maintains a meek and quiet spirit.

Because her words are consistent with her inner wisdom and godly character, her speech edifies and is neither negative nor critical. When differences of opinion arise, she does not argue, manipulate, or complain. Whenever she communicates with others, she refrains from gossip, slander, or idle talk.

"She looketh well to the ways of her household, and eateth not the bread of idleness" (v. 27).

A careful surveillance of the members in the household allows her to understand individual needs. She plans and prepares ahead of time to divert any crisis that might occur to ensure her family is carefree and content.

The bread of idleness is to eat food that has not been earned. The household operates by the rule that "If a man will not work, he shall not eat." If each person works well, they will eat well.

"Her children arise up, and call her blessed; her husband *also*, and he praiseth her" (v. 28).

"Arise up" gives the implication the children are older. As children mature, many appreciate the sacrificial service made on their behalf, but many do not. God is aware of the efforts a mother makes, and He will reward accordingly.

Her husband praises her because he is more aware than anyone else of the sacrifices she has made for the family. He is eager to boast about her because he is proud to be her husband, and when given the opportunity, he compliments her in public. He refuses to degrade her by making critical remarks or by making mention of her weaknesses and failures. When she is ill-spoken of by others, he is quick to come to her defense.

"Many daughters have done virtuously, but thou excellest them all" (v. 29).

This verse is the only one spoken by the husband. Because he sees her merits as exceeding those of any other woman, he values her as a rare gem, a woman fit for a king. Indeed, she is a special gift from God.

"Favour *is* deceitful, and beauty *is* vain: *but* a woman *that* feareth the Lord, she shall be praised" (v. 30).

The description of the virtuous woman never mentions physical attractiveness because virtue commands respect far more than beauty. *Matthew Henry's Commentary* makes a thought-provoking statement regarding beauty.

> Beauty is a fading thing at the best and therefore vain and deceitful. A fit of sickness will stain and sully it in a little time; a thousand accidents may blast this flower in its prime; old age will certainly wither it, and death and the grave consume it. But the fear of God reigning in the heart is the beauty of the soul; it recommends those that have it to the favour of God, and is, in his sight, of great price; it will last forever, and bid defiance to death itself, which consumes the beauty of the body, but consummates the beauty of the soul.[1]

A woman who fears the Lord has godly character because the fear of the Lord is the beginning of all wisdom. This woman has a genuine faith in Christ that gives her a fervent desire to love and please her Master. She is teachable so that she can be conformed to the image of

Jesus Christ and live a righteous life. The Bible is esteemed and obeyed as she maintains a close fellowship through prayer and worship.

"Give her of the fruit of her hands; and let her own works praise her in the gates" (v. 31).

The virtuous woman is usually too meek and humble to desire public attention, but she still should be given what she rightly deserves—the praise of others. Words of praise encourage the heart and motivate the spirit to continue the task.

"Let her own works praise her" indicates her turn has arrived to receive recognition in the gates. Her accomplishments have her name on them—not her husband's. If she is not praised in this world, she will be rewarded in Heaven.

Investigation

What are the most important inner qualities of the virtuous woman?

_____

_____

_____

_____

Why is physical beauty vain?

_____

_____

_____

_____

In Conclusion

The virtuous woman is an excellent example of modesty and godly character.

> If the virtuous woman is not praised
>
> in this world, she will be rewarded in Heaven.

O to Be Like Thee

O to be like Thee! Blessed Redeemer,
This is my constant longing and prayer;
Gladly I'll forfeit all of earth's treasures,
Jesus, Thy perfect likeness to wear.

Refrain:

O to be like Thee! O to be like Thee,
Blessed Redeemer, pure as Thou art!
Come in Thy sweetness; come in Thy fullness.
Stamp Thine own image deep on my heart.

O to be like Thee! Full of compassion,
Loving, forgiving, tender and kind,
Helping the helpless, cheering the fainting,
Seeking the wand'ring sinner to find!

O to be like Thee! While I am pleading,
Pour out Thy Spirit, fill with Thy love.
Make me a temple meet for Thy dwelling;
Fit me for life and heaven above.

— Thomas O. Chisholm

Lesson 12

Separation

Introduction

What does it mean to be separated from the world?

Illustration

Michelle was assigned a project in art class. First, she made two circles of white paint on the poster board. Next, with another paintbrush, she made a circle of black paint. Then she added one drop of black paint to one of the white circles and mixed the paint together. She watched closely as the white paint turned gray. Michelle could see the difference between the white and black circles that were separated, but in the circle where the paint was mixed together, she could no longer see a clear distinction between the two colors. As instructed, Michelle wrote down the number one on her paper to indicate that only one drop of black paint was needed to make the difference.

To finish her project, Michelle kept adding more drops of white paint to the gray circle. Although the gray color continued to lighten, she could not make the gray circle completely white again.

Insights

The same principle is true with sin. Like the single drop of black paint, one sin is all that is needed to infiltrate a person's life and damage their testimony for the Lord. *Gray* means "compromise," and God never intended for Christians to compromise with the ungodliness in the culture.

In the Old Testament, the Israelites polluted their lives with their worship of Baal and other false gods, which broke the first two of the Ten Commandments.

> Thou shalt have no other gods before me. Thou shalt not make unto thee any graven image, or any likeness *of any thing* that *is* in heaven above, or that *is* in the earth beneath, or that *is* in the water under the earth: Thou shalt not bow down thyself to them, nor serve them: for I the Lord thy God *am* a jealous God, visiting the iniquity of the fathers upon the children unto the third and fourth *generation* of them that hate me; And shewing mercy unto thousands of them that love me, and keep my commandments (Exodus 20:3–6).

God wanted the Israelites to worship only Him as a witness to the pagan nations around them. Despite God's commands, the Israelites committed idolatry by worshiping at the same pagan altars as their neighbors, and the line of separation disappeared.

One night God spoke to Solomon, a king in Israel, about the seriousness of turning away from the one true God. God gave Solomon a stern warning that if he obeyed God's commandments, the kingdom would prosper, but if he disobeyed God, the kingdom would be destroyed.

> But if ye turn away, and forsake my statutes and my commandments, which I have set before you, and shall go and serve other gods, and worship them; Then will I pluck them up by the roots out of my land which I have given them; and this house, which I have sanctified for my name, will I cast out of my sight, and will make it *to be* a proverb and a byword among all nations. And this

house, which is high, shall be an astonishment to every one that passeth by it; so that he shall say, Why hath the LORD done thus unto this land, and unto this house? And it shall be answered, Because they forsook the LORD God of their fathers, which brought them forth out of the land of Egypt, and laid hold on other gods, and worshipped them, and served them: therefore hath he brought all this evil upon them (2 Chronicles 7:19–22).

Solomon disobeyed when he married many foreign wives who turned his heart away from God. After Solomon died, Rehoboam rejected the advice of his father's older, wiser counselors and listened to his peers, which resulted in the division of the kingdom.

Instruction

Idols existed in Solomon's day, and idols still exist today. The idols in Solomon's day were images or representations of false gods that were the objects of their worship. Idolatry today can extend beyond physically bowing before images to harboring various idols in the heart.

Heart idolatry demands more time, money, emotions, or attention than is justifiable. Heart idolatry is self-centered instead of God-centered, which violates the command given in Deuteronomy 6:5 that states, "And thou shalt love the LORD thy God with all thine heart, and with all thy soul, and with all thy might."

Heart idolatry can be deceiving if nothing is sinful or wrong with the object or activity being practiced. There is a fine line between enjoyment and enslavement. Proper enjoyment limits the activity to the appropriate time and place, whereas enslavement gives preference to the idol to the extent of disobeying God by failing to give God priority in every area of life.

Another characteristic of heart idolatry is possessiveness. Since the mind rationalizes that nothing is morally wrong with the idol, there is an unwillingness to give up the attraction because the loss of enjoyment is too costly. The heart is so attached to the idol that if the idol were to be taken away, deep disappointment or even anger could erupt. To avoid the sin of idolatry, a diligent search of the heart is needed to determine the motive.

Investigation

Why are idols so deceptive and addictive?

_____

_____

_____

The word *world* in this lesson refers to the "satanic system of the culture which is evil and opposed to all that is righteous." The Bible commands Christians to be separated from the ungodliness that is in the world.

CHRISTIANS ARE TO LIVE IN THE WORLD BUT NOT LIVE LIKE THE WORLD.

"Wherefore come out from among them, and be ye separate, saith the Lord, and touch not the unclean *thing*; and I will receive you, And will be a Father unto you, and ye shall be my sons and daughters, saith the Lord Almighty" (2 Corinthians 6:17–18).

How can a Christian woman dress differently from the world if the selection of modest clothing is limited?

_____

_____

_____

_____

CHRISTIANS ARE NOT TO LOVE THE WORLD.

"Love not the world, neither the things *that are* in the world. If any man love the world, the love of the Father is not in him" (1 John 2:15).

How can a Christian woman discern if she is loving the things in the world?

_____

_____

CHRISTIANS ARE NOT TO BE CONFORMED TO THE WORLD.

"And be not conformed to this world: but be ye transformed by the renewing of your mind, that ye may prove what *is* that good, and acceptable, and perfect, will of God" (Romans 12:2).

How can a Christian woman's faithfulness to God be expressed by her choice of clothes?

_____

_____

CHRISTIANS ARE TO AVOID ALL APPEARANCE OF EVIL.

"Abstain from all appearance of evil" (1 Thessalonians 5:22).

In what ways can a Christian woman avoid the appearance of evil?

_____

_____

129

THE WORLD'S WAY OF LIVING
IS NOT OF GOD.

"For all that *is* in the world, the lust of the flesh, and the lust of the eyes, and the pride of life, is not of the Father, but is of the world" (1 John 2:16).

In what ways can a Christian woman not allow the lust of the eyes to influence her clothing choices?

_____

_____

_____

CHRISTIANS ARE TO KEEP THEMSELVES
UNSPOTTED FROM THE WORLD.

"Pure religion and undefiled before God and the Father is this, To visit the fatherless and widows in their affliction, *and* to keep himself unspotted from the world" (James 1:27).

What does "unspotted from the world" mean?

_____

_____

_____

Instruction

Biblical separation involves having contact with the world without being contaminated by sinful actions or attitudes. Since a Christian woman is to associate with the unsaved, she should be careful not to participate in any ungodly activities that could affect her testimony.

If a Christian woman does participate in a worldly practice, an unsaved woman might assume Christianity condones that action. Conversely, if the unsaved woman knows the Christian should not be participating in the practice, she could charge the Christian with hypocrisy. In either case, the Christian who does not model a different lifestyle loses an opportunity to demonstrate to the unsaved the difference Christ can make in a life.

God desires for a Christian woman to be an example by living a life worthy of emulation. Living a life according to higher standards can be difficult as others might misinterpret her motives and charge her with legalism or pride. Even when she is confident that her way of living pleases the Lord, criticism and rejection can still be hurtful.

In contrast, following the crowd is usually a convenient and pleasurable path. To adopt the standards of the majority provides a sense of acceptance at the time but can later lead to deep regrets. Furthermore, following others can cause a woman to make ungodly decisions that will damage her testimony for the Lord.

With regard to clothing, a woman should consider if she is influencing others to dress in a godly manner or if she is compromising with the world's standards. Is her motive primarily to please God or to please herself?

Insights

Proverbs 4:14–15 give the admonition to "Enter not into the path of the wicked, and go not in the way of evil *men*. Avoid it, pass not by it, turn from it, and pass away." Later in verses 26 and 27, the warning is reinforced: "Ponder the path of thy feet, and let all thy ways be established. Turn not to the right hand nor to the left: remove thy foot from evil."

In Conclusion

There is a delicate balance between living in the world and not living like the world.

> God never intended for Christians to
> compromise with the ungodliness in the culture.

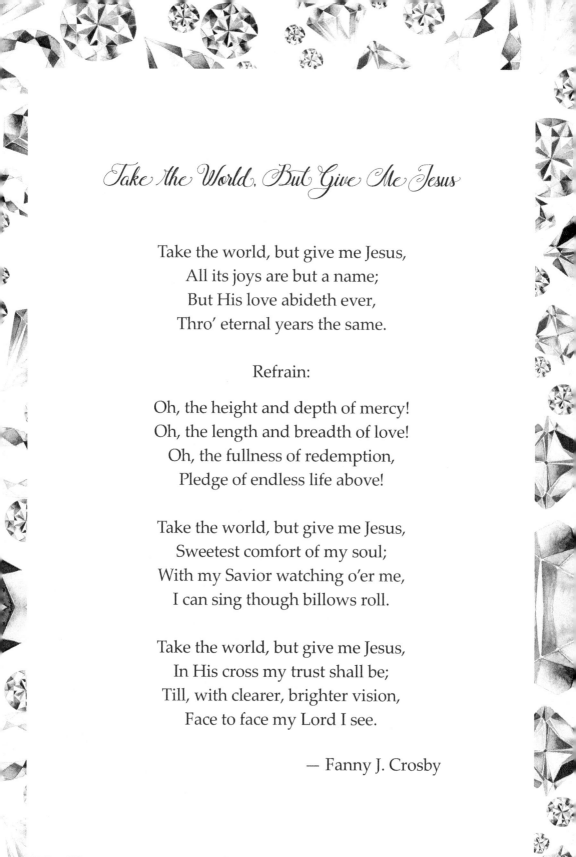

Take the World, But Give Me Jesus

Take the world, but give me Jesus,
All its joys are but a name;
But His love abideth ever,
Thro' eternal years the same.

Refrain:

Oh, the height and depth of mercy!
Oh, the length and breadth of love!
Oh, the fullness of redemption,
Pledge of endless life above!

Take the world, but give me Jesus,
Sweetest comfort of my soul;
With my Savior watching o'er me,
I can sing though billows roll.

Take the world, but give me Jesus,
In His cross my trust shall be;
Till, with clearer, brighter vision,
Face to face my Lord I see.

— Fanny J. Crosby

LESSON 13

Eye Magnets

Introduction

What types of clothing *magnetically* attract a man's eyes?

Illustration

After work, Olivia decided to stop at the boutique shop. As she browsed through the selection on the rack, she suddenly gasped, "A hot-pink bodycon dress!" She reached for the price tag and was thrilled to see the dress was on sale. "I just love the color," she whispered as she hurried to the changing room. After she struggled to get the dress on, Olivia gazed in the mirror. To her delight, the dress conformed tightly to her body so that her figure was clearly noticeable. "Super sexy!" she exclaimed.

Anxious to see the reactions of her co-workers, Olivia wore her new dress the next day. As she approached the office building, a group of workmen at a construction site nearby suddenly stopped talking and watched her until she was out of sight.

Why did her appearance captivate their attention?

Instruction

God created men and women to be different physically, mentally, and emotionally. Men are aroused by visual stimuli, whereas women are aroused by emotions and touch. Because of this, men notice the bodily appearance of women much more than women notice the bodily appearance of men. Because the man is a visual creature, he is keenly aware of how a woman is dressed. When a woman's clothes emphasize the size, shape, and curves of her body, a man's curiosity and sexual desires can be aroused. At that point, the battle can be a difficult one for him.

Unfortunately, some women disregard the fact that their appearance is seductive. Their retort is, "It's the man's problem." The man is ultimately accountable for his thoughts, but the woman must remember that she is responsible not to allure or entice a man by her appearance.

Perhaps a woman may not have the motive or desire to arouse lust. What she may not realize is that a man cannot see her motive, only her appearance. If she is dressed immodestly, she can be a temptation regardless of her motive.

Because each person has blind spots, learning to see through the eyes of others is important. To prevent being a temptation, a woman would be wise to request her husband's opinion about her appearance or to ask for advice from a mature Christian friend.

Other women may not realize the seriousness of their appearance because of their emotional needs. Since the media depicts women in tight, body-revealing attire as the epitome of female beauty, women feel they must adhere to this standard. The temptation is for a woman to adopt immodest clothing in hopes of feeling attractive enough for someone to love and accept her. A Christian woman should not use clothing for the purpose of self-fulfillment but should allow the Lord to meet her emotional needs. If she dresses with the motive of glorifying God, she will less likely be a temptation to men.

Investigation

Since men respond to visual stimuli, why would a woman not want to dress modestly to prevent temptation?

_____

_____

_____

Insights

The responsibility of a Christian man is to resist temptation as he relies on the power of the Holy Spirit to replace any sinful thoughts with truth from God's Word. Resisting temptation is not an easy task; in fact, every man has struggled with lust to some degree.

The Bible contains examples of men who controlled their physical passions and men who did not. Job's commitment to moral purity was evident when he vowed, "I made a covenant with mine eyes; why then should I think upon a maid?" (Job 31:1).

Job 1:1 describes Job as "perfect [undefiled] and upright, and one that feared God, and eschewed evil." *Eschew* is "to abstain from evil, both deliberately and habitually." Job was a man of integrity who deliberately avoided sin and consistently lived a righteous life; therefore, others could not accuse him of any moral failure.

Another example of a man who controlled his sexual passions was Joseph. Day after day he resisted the advances of his master's wife.

> And Joseph was brought down to Egypt; and Potiphar, an officer of Pharaoh, captain of the guard, an Egyptian, bought him of the hands of the Ishmeelites, which had brought him down thither. And the LORD was with Joseph, and he was a prosperous man; and he was in the house of his master the Egyptian. And his master saw that the LORD *was* with him, and that the LORD made all

that he did to prosper in his hand. And Joseph found grace in his sight, and he served him: and he made him overseer over his house, and all *that* he had he put into his hand. And it came to pass from the time *that* he had made him overseer in his house, and over all that he had, that the Lord blessed the Egyptian's house for Joseph's sake; and the blessing of the Lord was upon all that he had in the house, and in the field. And he left all that he had in Joseph's hand; and he knew not aught he had, save the bread which he did eat. And Joseph was *a* goodly *person*, and well favoured. And it came to pass after these things, that his master's wife cast her eyes upon Joseph; and she said, Lie with me. But he refused, and said unto his master's wife, Behold, my master wotteth not what *is* with me in the house, and he hath committed all that he hath to my hand; *There is* none greater in this house than I; neither hath he kept back any thing from me but thee, because thou *art* his wife: how then can I do this great wickedness, and sin against God? And it came to pass, as she spake to Joseph day by day, that he hearkened not unto her, to lie by her, *or* to be with her. And it came to pass about this time, that *Joseph* went into the house to do his business; and *there was* none of the men of the house there within. And she caught him by his garment, saying, Lie with me: and he left his garment in her hand, and fled, and got him out (Genesis 39:1–12).

Instruction

Joseph was a "goodly [attractive]" man, and Potiphar's wife was most likely a beautiful woman. *Matthew Henry's Commentary on the Whole Bible* explains that "Remarkable beauty, either of men or women, often proves a dangerous snare both to themselves and others."[1]

Even though Joseph and Potiphar's wife were both physically attractive, several contrasts between them should be considered. For example, Joseph was a slave and probably dressed in ordinary work clothes, whereas Potiphar's wife had the means to dress extravagantly since her husband was extremely wealthy.

Because Joseph was a diligent, conscientious worker, he efficiently managed the household and field. Potiphar's wife most likely had servants to perform all her tasks, giving her ample time to get bored and to feel lonely.

Although Joseph was given a substantial amount of responsibility, he remained a slave in rank. Potiphar's wife, no doubt, had been elevated to prominence since her husband was one of Pharaoh's high-ranking officials.

Joseph was focused on God's purpose for his life; thus, he remained faithful in his responsibilities. Potiphar's wife, however, was self-focused and sought only to satisfy her own fleshly desires by lusting after Joseph.

Even though Joseph was a young man with strong physical passions, he resisted sexual temptation. In contrast, Potiphar's wife yielded to lust and became shameful and aggressive. She offered sexual satisfaction, but Joseph viewed sin for what it is—a great wickedness against God.

Obviously, Joseph knew that a refusal to her forceful demand would cause offense because he had already refused her several times. To get revenge, Potiphar's wife shifted the blame to Joseph. She told her vicious lie to the servants of the house and repeated the accusation to her husband when he arrived home.

Perhaps Potiphar suspected that Joseph was innocent; nevertheless, he sentenced him to prison. Joseph may have lost his garment, but he never lost his character.

Investigation

Explain how "remarkable beauty" can be a snare.

_____

_____

_____

Why was Joseph able to resist temptation?

_____

_____

Insights

In contrast to Joseph who won the battle against lust, Samson lost the battle with lust.

> And Samson went down to Timnath, and saw a woman in Timnath of the daughters of the Philistines. And he came up, and told his father and his mother, and said, I have seen a woman in Timnath of the daughters of the Philistines: now therefore get her for me to wife. Then his father and his mother said unto him, *Is there* never a woman among the daughters of thy brethren, or among all my people, that thou goest to take a wife of the uncircumcised Philistines? And Samson said unto his father, Get her for me; for she pleaseth me well (Judges 14:1–3).

Instruction

Samson went into enemy territory and was physically attracted to a Philistine woman, so he implored his father and mother to get her for his wife. Samson's parents objected to the marriage because the Philistines were one of Israel's greatest enemies; nevertheless, he proceeded to coerce his father to get the woman for him.

Later, Samson traveled into Philistine territory again and loved a woman named Delilah (Judges 16:4). The Philistines hated Samson and sought revenge because he had destroyed some of their main crops and killed many of their men. The lords of the Philistines each promised Delilah eleven hundred pieces of silver to find out the secret of Samson's strength. Delilah nagged Samson until he revealed the truth.

> There hath not come a razor upon mine head; for I *have been* a Nazarite unto God from my mother's womb: if I be shaven, then my strength will go from me, and I shall become weak, and be like any *other* man (Judges 16:17).

While Samson was asleep on Delilah's knees, she called in one of the Philistines to cut Samson's hair. At the moment his Nazarite vow was broken, God departed from him. The Philistines captured Samson, blinded him, and transported him to Gaza where he was humiliated as he toiled at the grinding mill, doing work usually assigned to slaves, women, or donkeys.

Since the Israelites were commanded not to marry or have relationships with pagan women, Samson paid a high price for his disobedience. Samson's wrong choices are a lesson to Christian girls not to go among the unsaved to find a mate, for once passions are ignited, reasoning is usually to no avail.

Second Corinthians 6:14 warns, "Be ye not unequally yoked [joined] together with unbelievers: for what fellowship hath righteousness with unrighteousness? and what communion [oneness of spirit] hath light with darkness?" A man's character and relationship to God are far more important than physical appearance.

Investigation

How can a Christian girl or woman discern if a man possesses godly character?

_____

_____

_____

Insights

Another sad story of moral failure is David, one of Israel's kings.

> And it came to pass, after the year was expired, at the time when kings go forth *to battle*, that David sent Joab, and his servants with him, and all Israel; and they destroyed the children of Ammon, and besieged Rabbah. But David tarried still at Jerusalem. And it came to pass in an eveningtide, that David arose from off his bed, and walked upon the roof of the king's house: and from the roof he saw a woman washing herself; and the woman *was* very beautiful to look upon. And David sent and enquired after the woman. And *one* said, *Is* not this Bath-sheba, the daughter of Eliam, the wife of Uriah the Hittite? And David sent messengers, and took her; and she came in unto him, and he lay with her; for she was purified from her uncleanness: and she returned unto her house. And the woman conceived, and sent and told David, and said, I *am* with child (2 Samuel 11:1–5).

Instruction

David was not an ungodly man since God called him "a man after mine own heart" (Acts 13:22). This passage contains many lessons for men, but one lesson for women to learn is the power the female body has to excite the sexual passions of any man, even a spiritual man. When the sexual passions of a man are excited, he is more apt to make unwise decisions. Many men have damaged their reputations, lost their families, and lost their ministries by yielding to lust. Even if the sin is forgiven, the consequences can continue indefinitely.

David's uncontrolled passion led to a series of sinful acts: Bathsheba's adultery, her pregnancy, and her husband's death when he was moved to the front of the hottest battle (2 Samuel 11:15). Later, the prophet Nathan proclaimed God's judgment upon David by announcing, "Now therefore the sword shall never depart from thine house; because thou hast despised me, and hast taken the wife of Uriah the Hittite to be thy wife" (12:10). Then David confessed, "I have sinned against the Lord" (12:13a).

After David's confession, Nathan prophesied, "Howbeit, because by this deed thou hast given great occasion to the enemies of the Lord to blaspheme, the child also *that is* born unto thee shall surely die" (12:14). The child did die as Nathan had predicted.

The consequences of David's sin resulted in the rape of his daughter, Tamar, the murder of his son Amnon, the blatant act of his son Absalom going in unto his father's concubines, and the subsequent rebellion and death of Absalom. David experienced the well-known saying, "Sin will take you farther than you want to go, keep you longer than you want to stay, and cost you more than you want to pay."

Eye Magnets

Eye magnets are "ways a woman dresses that attract a man's eyes and create the potential for impure thoughts and lust." Each of the following eye magnets listed can affect men differently, but they all have the potential to be a temptation for sin.

This section is not intended to be a legalistic list of dos and don'ts. The information is shared to help women understand men and to know what types and styles of clothes should be avoided to prevent temptation.

A man's eyes tend to gravitate to a woman's body when her size and shape are revealed by tight clothing. Stretchy material has a tendency to cling to the body and emphasize the breasts, buttocks, and crotch area. The fashion industry admits that tight clothing is designed for the very purpose of emphasizing the body in a sensual manner. To prevent temptation, loose garments are better.

Exposed skin can be teasing to the man because it can awaken his curiosity and stimulate the desire to see more. Garments such as strapless dresses, spaghetti strap dresses, one shoulder dresses, cold shoulder dresses, backless dresses, distressed clothing, and a lace dress with skin showing through can all be tempting. Clothing that exposes the upper thigh can also be tempting.

When a man sees the cleavage of a woman's breasts, even a little bit, he can be tempted to use his imagination to complete the picture even though some of the information cannot be seen. This is called the Law of Closure. The Law of Closure states that when parts of a whole picture are missing, perception fills in the visual gap. Because the brain is intrigued by an incomplete picture, the mind will always pause to finish an unfinished picture.

Women do not realize how tempting long slits are whether in the front, on the side, or in the back. The movement of a woman walking causes the slit to open and close visually. As the garment opens, men can see the leg, and when the garment closes with the next step, they cannot. No wonder men call this type of skirt a "peek-a-boo skirt."

The material of a sheer blouse is so thin and translucent that a man can partially see the woman's undergarments, especially if the blouse is white and the underwear black. In addition, a woman may not realize that a sleeveless dress often exposes her underwear straps in the back as she moves her arm. Seeing underwear in public can arouse a man's imagination and spark impure thoughts.

Sometimes a dress or blouse may appear modest, but when the woman leans forward, she has no idea how much she has exposed to those in front of her. When bending forward, if a woman will deliberately place her hand at the top of her dress or blouse, she can save herself from indecent exposure.

Instruction

Am I responsible for my brother? Philippians 2:4 challenges the believer to "Look not every man on his own things, but every man also on the things of others." Galatians 5:13 adds, "For, brethren, ye have been called unto liberty; only *use* not liberty for an occasion to the flesh, but by love serve one another." To serve others includes encouraging spiritual growth. A woman's appearance should provide an atmosphere where men are not tempted and can maintain purity in their walk with the Lord.

First Corinthians 8:9 warns, "But take heed lest by any means this liberty of yours become a stumbling block to them that are weak." Many men were involved in sexual sin or pornography before they were saved; consequently, the sight of an immodest woman can be a strong temptation and a reminder of their sinful past. They have a spiritual desire not to sin, but their flesh is weak.

Love motivates a woman to yield her rights so that she will not offend a brother. What may be perfectly all right for her may be wrong in the eyes of someone else. Although she may not consider her appearance to be a temptation, someone else could. A woman who has yielded her rights will gladly give up her own desires so as not to cause a brother to stumble.

Richard Baxter, a great English pastor and theologian in the seventeenth century, warned women about the power of eye magnets.

> And though it be their sin and vanity that is the cause, it is nevertheless your sin to be the unnecessary occasion: for you must consider that you live among diseased souls! And you must not lay a stumbling-block in their way, nor blow up the fire of their lust, nor make your ornaments their snares; but you must walk among sinful persons, as you would do with a candle among straw or gunpowder; or else you may see the flame which you would not foresee, when it is too late to quench it.[2]

In Conclusion

Eye magnets cause men to be tempted and create the potential for lust.

A man cannot see a woman's motive, only her appearance. If she is dressed immodestly, she can be a temptation regardless of her motive.

Keep Thyself Pure

Keep thyself pure! Christ's soldier true,
Thro' life's loud strife He calls to you.
Thy Captain speaks: His Word obey;
So shall thy strength be as thy day.

Keep thyself pure! When lusts assail.
When flesh is strong and spirit frail,
Fight on, a fadeless crown, to win
Christ will give vic-t'ry over sin.

O Holy Spirit, keep us pure,
Grant us Thy strength when sins allure;
Our bodies are Thy temple, Lord;
Be Thou in thought and act adored.

— S. M. Plumptre

LESSON 14

God's Purpose for Clothing

Introduction

What is the purpose of clothing?

Illustration

Sarah was burdened for the ladies in her neighborhood since none of them attended church. After she discussed her concern with her husband, she decided to invite them to her house for a Tuesday evening Bible study. Her husband graciously agreed to take care of Jimmy, their two-year-old toddler, for the evening.

As the women began to arrive, Daddy ushered Jimmy upstairs for his bath. Just as Daddy finished the bath and began gathering up the toys, Jimmy decided he wanted to give Mommy a good-night hug. Daddy wrapped a dry towel around him, and Jimmy eagerly headed for the stairs. As he rushed down the stairs, the towel loosened, and by the time he reached the last step, the towel dropped off. Jimmy ran naked in front of the ladies to Mommy.

Why was Jimmy not embarrassed?

Insights

CLOTHING: A PROVISION FROM GOD

"And they were both naked, the man and his wife, and were not ashamed" (Genesis 2:25). God created Adam and Eve as perfect individuals, and they lived in a perfect environment where they enjoyed perfect fellowship with Him. Although they were without sin, God created them with the capacity to obey or not to obey.

> And when the woman saw that the tree *was* good for food, and that it *was* pleasant to the eyes, and a tree to be desired to make *one* wise, she took of the fruit thereof, and did eat, and gave also unto her husband with her; and he did eat. And the eyes of them both were opened, and they knew that they *were* naked; and they sewed fig leaves together, and made themselves aprons (Genesis 3:6–7).

God instructed Adam and Eve not to eat of the tree of the knowledge of good and evil, but they chose to disobey. The consequences were more serious than just eating a piece of fruit: Eve believed Satan's lie, Adam disobeyed God's instruction, their innocent state was lost, sin entered into the whole human race, and man has suffered the effects and consequences of sin ever since.

After their eyes were opened, their new knowledge of good and evil was not as advantageous as Satan had promised. When they saw their nakedness for the first time, they experienced a deep sense of guilt and shame that caused them to instinctively know their bodies needed to be covered. Even though Adam and Eve attempted to hide their physical nakedness, the real issue was that their relationship with God had been severed. In love, God took the initiative to search for them.

> And they heard the voice of the Lᴏʀᴅ God walking in the garden in the cool of the day: and Adam and his wife hid themselves from the presence of the Lᴏʀᴅ God amongst the trees of the garden. And the Lᴏʀᴅ God called unto Adam, and said unto him, Where *art* thou? And he said, I heard thy voice in the garden, and I was afraid, because I *was* naked; and I hid myself. And he said, Who told thee that thou *wast* naked? Hast thou eaten of the tree, whereof I commanded thee that thou shouldest not eat? (Genesis 3:8–11).

Adam and Eve's attempt to hide among the trees was futile. "I was naked" was Adam's feeble excuse, but modesty was not the real issue. They hid themselves because of their sin and the inevitable punishment they feared would follow. God's rhetorical questions were not meant to obtain information but to confront Adam with his disobedience.

Adam and Eve's sin was a serious matter to God. Although His justice required Him to impose a penalty for their sin, His mercy and grace allowed the couple to be restored to fellowship with Him.

From God's perspective, Adam and Eve's hasty fig leaf aprons indicated their total inability to atone for their sin. God then provided them with garments that were acceptable to Him. "Unto Adam also and to his wife did the Lᴏʀᴅ God make coats of skins, and clothed them" (Genesis 3:21).

The "coats of skins" came from the death of animals because "without shedding of blood is no remission [forgiveness]" (Hebrews 9:22b). God was instructing Adam and Eve that there had to be a payment for their sin that required bloodshed and death. These animal sacrifices pointed to Jesus Christ who would one day come to earth to die on a cross and shed His blood as the perfect, sinless sacrifice for man's sin once and for all.

Investigation

Why did God use animal skins to clothe Adam and Eve's bodies?

_____

_____

_____

Why did God Himself offer the sacrifice instead of Adam and Eve?

_____

_____

_____

Instruction

CLOTHING: A DETERRENT TO SIN

When man disobeyed God in the garden of Eden, his sinless state was lost, and sin passed on to the whole human race. "Wherefore, as by one man sin entered into the world, and death by sin; and so death passed upon all men, for that all have sinned" (Romans 5:12). Man was now in bondage to his sin nature to obey its fleshly desires. The fact that Adam and Eve knew right away that they were naked was indicative that, from that moment on, physical passions and lust would always be a struggle. Therefore, to deter sin, man's body needed to be clothed.

Although nudists might consider themselves to be in a natural state of innocence like Adam and Eve experienced in the garden of Eden, nudity cannot be considered innocence. Public nudity is an act of disobedience against God because man is deliberately removing the clothing God commanded him to wear.

Clothing is a deterrent to sin only if it conceals the body, not exposes the body. Modesty cannot totally eliminate all the sinful thoughts in a man's mind, but modest, loose clothing can greatly deter those thoughts from happening.

SPIRITUAL CLOTHING:
A PREREQUISITE FOR HEAVEN

To enter Heaven, a woman must be clothed with the spiritual garments mentioned in Isaiah 61:10.

> I will greatly rejoice in the LORD, my soul shall be joyful in my God; for he hath clothed me with the garments of salvation, he hath covered me with the robe of righteousness, as a bridegroom decketh *himself* with ornaments, and as a bride adorneth *herself* with her jewels.

A woman can receive the "garments of salvation" when she is convicted that she is a lost sinner who is destined for eternal punishment in Hell. She must realize that she can only be saved by God's grace and not by any good works that she has done. She must believe that Christ died on the cross to pay the penalty for her sin, was buried, and rose again the third day to give her eternal life. After she has truly repented of her sin, she should ask God to forgive her. Then she can invite Jesus Christ into her life to be her Lord and Savior.

Because of Christ's death on the cross as the payment for sin, the Christian woman is given Christ's righteousness as the substitute for her unrighteousness. When God looks upon her, He sees her as cleansed and forgiven. After being saved, a Christian woman should continue to walk daily in Christ's righteousness. "But put ye on the Lord Jesus Christ, and make not provision for the flesh, to *fulfill* the lust *thereof*" (Romans 13:14).

The last part of Isaiah 61:10 is an analogy that compares the garments of salvation to the finest attire of a bride and groom adorned for their wedding. Christ is the bridegroom, and the church, which includes all born-again believers, is His bride. Someday there will be a glorious wedding celebration in Heaven. Do you know for sure you will be there?

In Conclusion

Only those who belong to Christ wear the spiritual garments of salvation and His robe of righteousness.

> There must be a payment for sin that requires bloodshed and death.

His Robes for Mine

His robes for mine: O wonderful exchange!
Clothed in my sin, Christ suffered 'neath God's rage.
Draped in His righteousness, I'm justified.
In Christ I live, for in my place He died.

Refrain:

I cling to Christ and marvel at the cost:
Jesus forsaken; God estranged from God.
Bought by such love, my life is not my own:
My praise—my all—shall be for Christ alone.

His robes for mine: what cause have I for dread?
God's daunting Law Christ mastered in my stead.
Faultless I stand with righteous works not mine,
Saved by my Lord's vicarious death and life.

His robes for mine: God's justice is appeased.
Jesus is crushed, and thus the Father's pleased.
Christ drank God's wrath on sin then cried, "'Tis done!"
Sin's wage is paid; propitiation won.

His robes for mine: such anguish none can know.
Christ, God's beloved, condemned as though His foe.
He, as though I, accursed and left alone;
I, as though He, embraced and welcomed home!

— Chris Anderson

The End of the Journey

The time has come to review the material that has been studied. The journey began in Lesson 1 by establishing the fact that clothing communicates a message without a word being spoken. Since fashion designers understand this concept, they use the tactics of skimpiness, tightness, sensuality, and purpose to communicate their values and lifestyles.

In Lesson 2, attention was turned from fashion designers to God's Word. A diligent study of 1 Timothy 2 and Titus 2 expounded upon God's definition of genuine beauty. The lesson summarized the truth that a godly character and modest apparel give a woman a beauty that all the best cosmetics and expensive clothing in the world cannot duplicate.

Lesson 3 focused on the most important key to modesty—the heart. Women were exhorted to diligently guard their hearts because a woman's goals, ambitions, and desires can affect her choice of clothing; therefore, clothing can be a mirror of the heart.

Since legalism is often misunderstood, Lesson 4 refuted these wrong concepts: the attempt to earn salvation by good works, the strict adherence to rules to produce spiritual growth, and the elevation of personal standards and preferences to the level of biblical absolutes. Lesson 5 concluded that the motive in a woman's heart determines whether or not she is legalistic.

In Lesson 6, blurred vision was defined as having a wrong view of God. When a woman has a wrong view of God, she will likely have a wrong view of modesty because only God has the authority to define modesty. A right view of God's holiness and lordship should result in modesty.

Lesson 7 provided factors that might contribute to the development of an immoral woman. The account of the Samaritan woman at the well gave hope that Christ can satisfy the inner desires of the heart and transform any life.

Next, Lesson 8 examined the characteristics of the adulterous wife in Proverbs 7 and Gomer in the book of Hosea. Any believer can commit spiritual adultery if they succumb to the sinful lifestyle of the world. God's heart is grieved whenever a believer sins, but He is faithful to forgive if only the believer will repent.

Lesson 9 taught that clothes can be a revealer of inner character. Examples of ungodly women were the daughters of Zion and the wicked Jezebel. According to King Solomon in Proverbs 11:22, a beautiful woman without discretion is compared to a gold ring in a pig's nose that gets subjected to dirt and filth.

In contrast, a study was made in Lesson 10 of the moral qualities a woman possesses and how they relate to modesty. Biblical examples of godly character included Abigail, Esther, and Ruth.

Lesson 11 expounded upon the characteristics and qualities of the virtuous woman in Proverbs 31. The passage never mentions beauty because holiness and virtue command respect far more than physical attractiveness.

The journey continued in Lesson 12 with a study on separation. God desires for a Christian to be an example of godliness among the unsaved by not allowing idols to control the heart. Heart idolatry was defined as an activity or object that takes more time, money, emotions, or attention than is justifiable, making that part of the life self-centered instead of God-centered.

In Lesson 13, a contrast was made between Job and Joseph who resisted temptation and Samson and David who yielded to temptation. Explanations were given on the different types and styles of garments that can be a temptation for men. Key biblical principles were provided to assist women in their choice of clothing.

The journey concluded in Lesson 14 with a discussion on clothing in the past, present, and future. God gave Adam and Eve coats from animal skins to show that a blood sacrifice was needed to cover their sin, and adequate clothing is essential today because of the evil that is in man's heart. Only those who know Christ personally wear the spiritual garments required for Heaven.

In the Bible, God gives His principles for modesty, so I have sought diligently to present truth based upon His Word. My prayer is that the seed of God's Word will fall upon good soil and produce much fruit for His glory.

— Dorothy Zimmerman

DOROTHY ZIMMERMAN has been a pastor's wife for forty-nine years. Her teaching experience includes Sunday school, ladies' Bible studies, vacation Bible school, children's programs, and home schooling her four children.

Her creativity developed during the years she wrote mother-daughter banquet programs, women's missionary programs, and puppet skits using sixteen animal and people puppets that she created.

Endnotes

Lesson 1: The Designers' Tactics

1. Wikipedia contributors, "History of Swimwear 19th Century," *Wikipedia, The Free Encyclopedia,* accessed May 30, 2017, https://en.wikipedia.org/w/index.php?title=History_ of_ swimwear&oldid=917086986.

2. Wikipedia contributors, "History of Swimwear Early 20th Century," *Wikipedia, The Free Encyclopedia,* accessed May 30, 2017, https://en.wikipedia.org/w/index.php?title=History_ of_ swimwear&oldid=917086986.

3. Wikipedia contributors, "History of Swimwear 1910s," *Wikipedia, The Free Encyclopedia,* accessed May 30, 2017, https://en.wikipedia.org/w/index.php?title=History_ of_ swimwear&oldid=917086986.

4. ELLE By ELLE, "The History of the Bikini," accessed May 30, 2017, https://www.elle.com/fashion/g2906/the-history-of-the-bikini-654900/.

5. Rare Historical Photos, "Women Being Arrested for Wearing One Piece Bathing Suits," accessed May 30, 2017, https://rarehistoricalphotos.com/women-arrested-bathing-suits-1920s.

6. Wikipedia contributors, "History of Swimwear 1930s," *Wikipedia, The Free Encyclopedia,* accessed May 30, 2017, https://en.wikipedia.org/w/index.php?title=History_ of_ swimwear&oldid=917086986.

7.   Wikipedia contributors, "History of Swimwear 1940s," *Wikipedia, The Free Encyclopedia,* accessed May 30, 2017, https://en.wikipedia.org/w/index.php?title=History_ of_ swimwear&oldid=917086986.

8.   Wikipedia contributors, "Louis Réard,"*Wikipedia, The Free Encyclopedia,* accessed May 30, 2017, https://en.wikipedia. org/w/index.php?title= Louis_R%C3%A9ard&oldid=961564826.

9.   Wikipedia contributors, "Thong," *Wikipedia, The Free Encyclopedia,* accessed March 1, 2021, https://en.wikipedia. org/w/index.php?title=Thong&oldid=1006319763.

10. Isabel Wilkinson, "The Story Behind Brooke Shield's Famous Calvin Klein Jeans," *The New York Times Style Magazine,* December 2, 2015, accessed May 30, 2017, https://www. nytimes.com/2015 /12/02/t-magazine/fashion/brooke-shields-calvin-klein-jeans-ad-eighties.html.

11. Allyson Payer, "The Little-Known History of Leggings," accessed May 17, 2017, https://www.whowhatwear.com/ history-of-leggings-trend#:~:text=Following%20the%20 invention%20 of%20Lycra,the%20decade's%20mod%20 shift%20dresses.

12. Alison Adburgham, "Mary Quant," *The Guardian*, October 10, 1967, accessed May 17, 2017, https://www.theguardian.com/ century /1960-1969/Story/0,106475,00.html.

13. Calvin Klein, "About Calvin Klein, Inc.," accessed July 29, 2017, https://www.explore.calvinklein.com/en_US/corporate.html.

14. Vivienne Westwood, "Vivienne Westwood Quotes," BrainyQuote, accessed May 30, 2017, https://www.brainyquote. com/quotes /authors/v/vivienne_westwood.html.

15. Alexander McQueen, "Alexander McQueen Quotes," BrainyQuote, accessed May 30, 2017, https://www.brainyquote. com/quotes /authors/a/alexander_mcqueen.html.

16. Katherine Bernard, "Photos: Ten Most Rebellious Moments in Fashion," *Vogue*, accessed January 30, 2018, https://www. vogue.com/slideshow/ten-most-rebellious-moments-in-fashion.html.

17. Tommy Hilfiger, "Tommy Hilfiger Quotes," BrainyQuote, accessed May 17, 2017, https://www.brainyquote.com/quotes / quotes/t/tommyhilfi417085.html.

18. Kasturi Roy, "20 Powerful Ralph Lauren Quotes That Will 'Style' Your Life," *Lifehack*, accessed May 17, 2017, https://www. lifehack.org/articles/communication/20-powerful-ralph-lauren-quotes-that-will-style-your-life.html.

19. Wikipedia contributors, "Low-rise pants," *Wikipedia, The Free Encyclopedia*, accessed January 7, 2018, https://en.wikipedia.org/ w/index.php?title=Low-rise_pants&oldid=917524122.

20. Wikipedia contributors, "Le Smoking," *Wikipedia, The Free Encyclopedia*, accessed January 30, 2018, https://en.wikipedia. org/w/index.php?title=Le_ Smoking&oldid=907086798.

21. Pierre Cardin, "Pierre Cardin Quotes," BrainyQuote, accessed May 30, 2017, https://www.brainyquote.com/quotes/authors/p/ pierre_ cardin.html.

Lesson 6: Blurred Vision

1. David Vaughan and Diane Vaughan, *The Beauty of Modesty*, (Nashville: Cumberland House Publishing, 2005), 155.

2. Warren W. Wiersbe, *The Wiersbe Bible Commentary NT*, (Colorado Springs: David C. Cook, 2007), 356.

Lesson 7: The Immoral Woman

1. F. E. Longley, *The Home Circle, The Home World and Sunday School Companion*, Vol. I, No. 1, accessed May 12, 2018, (London: F. E. Longley, 1879), 17.

Lesson 11: The Virtuous Woman

1. Matthew Henry, *Matthew Henry's Commentary on the Whole Bible*, (Peabody: Hendrickson Publishers, 1991), 1027.

Lesson 13: Eye Magnets

1. Henry, 80.

2. Richard Baxter, *A Christian Directory in Baxter's Practical Works Vol I*, (London: George Virtue. Reprint, Ligonier: Soli Deo Gloria Publications, 1990), 392.

Bibliography

Anderson, Chris. "His Robes for Mine." *Rejoice Hymns*. Greenville: Majesty Music, 2011.

Baxter, Richard. *A Christian Directory in Baxter's Practical Works.* Vol I. London: George Virtue. Reprint, Ligonier: Soli Deo Gloria Publications, 1990.

Beaver, Jerry, and Heidi Beaver. *Christian Modesty: A Matter of the Heart*. Pleasant Prairie: Baptist Growth Publications, 2010.

Bishop, John, and Donna Bishop. *The Witness of Your Wardrobe.* Murfreesboro: Sword of the Lord Publishers, 2009.

Bliss, Philip P. "Once for All!" *Living Hymns*. Greenville: Better Music Publications, 1988.

Chisholm, Thomas O. "O to Be Like Thee." *Hymns for the Living Church*. Carol Stream: Hope Publishing Company, 1974.

Clark, Adam LL.D., F.S.A. *The Holy Bible with a Commentary and Critical Notes* Vol III. New York: Abingdon Press, no date.

Cloud, David. *Dressing for the Lord*. Port Huron: Way of Life Literature, 2008.

Crosby, Fanny J. "Take the World, but Give Me Jesus." *Living Hymns*. Greenville: Better Music Publications, 1988.

DeMoss, Nancy Leigh. *The Look: Does God Really Care What I Wear?* Niles: Revive Our Hearts, 2010.

Handford, Elizabeth Rice. *Your Clothes Say It for You.* Murfreesboro: Sword of the Lord Publishers, 1976.

Henry, Matthew. *Matthew Henry's Commentary on the Whole Bible.* Peabody: Hendrickson Publishers, 1991.

Hoffman, Elisha A. "Is Thy Heart Right with God?" *Living Hymns.* Greenville: Better Music Publications, 1988.

Kidd, David. *The Fall and Rise of Christian Standards: Thinking Biblically About Dress and Appearance.* Maitland: Xulon Press, 2005.

Life Application Study Bible. Carol Stream: Tyndale House Publishers, 1996.

Palmer, Horatio R. "Yield Not to Temptation." *Hymns for the Living Church.* Carol Stream: Hope Publishing Company, 1974.

Peace, Martha, and Kent Keller. *MODESTY: More Than a Change of Clothes.* Phillipsburg: P&R Publishing Company, 2015.

Plumptre, S. M. "Keep Thyself Pure." *Living Hymns.* West Columbia: Al Smith Ministries, 2012.

Pollard, Adelaide A. "Have Thine Own Way, Lord." *Hymns of the Christian Life.* Harrisburg: Christian Publications, Inc., 1936.

Poole, Matthew. *Matthew Poole's Commentary on the Holy Bible* Vol. II. Peabody: Hendrickson Publishers, 1984.

Rowe, James. "I Would Be Like Jesus." *Hymns of the Christian Life.* Harrisburg: Christian Publications, Inc., 1936.

Ryrie, Charles Caldwell, Th.D., Ph.D. *Ryrie Study Bible.* Chicago: Moody Publishers, 1994.

Scott, Clara H. "Open My Eyes, That I May See." *Living Hymns.* Greenville: Better Music Publications, 1988.

Toplady, Augustus M. "Rock of Ages, Cleft for Me." *Living Hymns.* Greenville: Better Music Publications, 1988.

Van DeVenter, Judson W. "I Surrender All." *Living Hymns.* Greenville: Better Music Publications, 1988.

Vaughan, David, and Diane Vaughan. *The Beauty of Modesty: Cultivating Virtue in the Face of a Vulgar Culture.* Nashville: Cumberland House Publishing, 2005.

Voke, Leonard C. "Can Others See Jesus in You?" *Living Hymns.* West Columbia: Al Smith Ministries, 2012.

Wiersbe, Warren W. *The Wiersbe Bible Commentary NT.* Colorado Springs: David C. Cook, 2007.

Wilkinson, Kate B. "May the Mind of Christ, My Savior." *Living Hymns.* Greenville: Better Music Publications, 1988.

Williams, Clara T. "Satisfied." *Hymns for the Living Church.* Carol Stream: Hope Publishing Company, 1974.

Made in the USA
Middletown, DE
26 March 2023

26887534R00097